ALBANIAN ASSIGNMENT

Published by Sapere Books.
20 Windermere Drive, Leeds, England, LS17 7UZ,
United Kingdom

saperebooks.com

Copyright © The Estate of David Smiley, 1984.
First published by Chatto & Windus, 1984.
The Estate of David Smiley has asserted their right to be identified as the author of this work.
All rights reserved.

No part of this publication may be reproduced, stored in any retrieval system, or transmitted, in any form, or by any means, electronic, mechanical, photocopying, recording, or otherwise, without the prior written permission of the publishers.

eBook ISBN: 978-1-913518-79-0.

ALBANIAN ASSIGNMENT

David Smiley

*To my Albanian friends,
alive and dead.*

Table of Contents

Chapter I: MO4   9
Chapter II: Briefing in Cairo   16
Chapter III: Drop into Greece and move to the Albanian frontier   25
Chapter IV: First partisan contacts and action   38
Chapter V: Supply drops and our first success   62
Chapter VI: Formation of 1st Partisan Brigade, retreat, Italian surrender   87
Chapter VII: Arrival of 'Trotsky's' mission and our evacuation   107
Chapter VIII: Operation 'Concensus II'   131
Chapter IX: Civil War   151
Chapter X: On the run and evacuation   172
Chapter XI: Postscript on Albania   205
Acknowledgements   213

Chapter I: MO4

My first steps towards Albania resulted from a chance meeting with Billy McLean, of the Royal Scots Greys, on a troopship in the Red Sea. In 1940, we were both members of a group of officers from the 1st Cavalry Division in Palestine who had volunteered to join the Somaliland Camel Corps, then hard-pressed by the Italians, who had invaded British Somaliland. Our ship arrived at Berbera on the day that it was decided to evacuate the colony so, staying only long enough to embark a number of evacuees and receive several Italian air raids, the convoy steamed back to Suez.

McLean and I shared our feelings about the war at that time. We feared that our horsed cavalry regiments in Palestine would never be used for more than internal security. To see more action, we would have to find employment in more active units, so we both decided to go to Cairo rather than obey the order to return to our regiments. Our plan worked.

McLean joined an organization known as MO4 and was sent with Colonels Wingate and Sandford to organize Abyssinian irregulars to fight the Italians. I called on General Archie Wavell, an old friend of my family, who was commanding the troops in Egypt and explained my problem to him. With his advice and help I joined the Middle East Commandos, who were just being formed.

Our Commando, No. 52 Middle East, was sent to the Sudan where we were based on the Abyssinian border near Gallabat, under the command of a Brigadier Bill Slim — later Field Marshal Lord Slim. We operated behind the Italian lines in Abyssinia, carrying out long-range patrols and ambushes on the enemy supply lines. Later we were withdrawn to Alexandria, where we guarded the docks. While there, I heard that my regiment was about to go into action in Iraq, and with some others of my unit we successfully applied to be allowed to rejoin it. That was a stroke of luck, because my commando was soon disbanded after being killed off or put in the bag in Crete.

I rejoined my regiment, the 1st Household Cavalry Regiment, just after they had been mechanized and in time to raise the siege of Habbaniya and push on to Baghdad. After the campaigns in Syria and Persia, I went in February 1942 with a squadron to the Western Desert. We were equipped with dummy tanks, which provoked our fair share of attacks from the German Stuka dive bombers. We were not sorry to be sent back to Cairo just before Rommel broke through our lines, captured Tobruk, and pressed on to the Egyptian frontier.

After a few days leave in Cairo, we went back to our regiment in Cyprus. I had met McLean again in Cairo. Just back from Abyssinia, he told me that his organization was recruiting officers to parachute into the Balkans to help the resistance movements against the German and Italian armies of occupation. He suggested that I join him. I was not keen to do so at that moment as the regiment was being equipped with armoured cars, and it was rumoured that they were to be sent to the Western Desert. The rumour was true, and we arrived in the desert to find ourselves acting as the armoured car screen to 13 Corps, commanded by General Brian Horrocks. After the breakthrough at Alamein we pushed ahead, collecting thousands of Italian prisoners, having occasional shoot-outs with pockets of German or Italian resistance, and passing vast quantities of abandoned enemy guns, tanks, vehicles and equipment.

Our morale was high, so it was a bitter disappointment when we were ordered not only to halt our pursuit, but to withdraw from the desert and return to Cairo. We did not appreciate at the time that there was not enough petrol and other supplies for the entire 8th Army to continue the advance, and we were among the unlucky ones who had to give up the chase.

While in Cairo, we had heard that we were to be sent up to the Syrian-Turkish border in case the Germans decided to thrust through Turkey into Syria and Palestine, and so threaten Egypt in the rear. I felt this was unlikely and I was depressed at the thought of again missing the war, so I sought out McLean and this time I told him I was keen to join him in MO4. He immediately arranged for me to be interviewed, and I was questioned by various officers including a Major Basil Davidson.

McLean had advised me that any battle experience or knowledge of explosives or guerrilla warfare would help in my interviews. My qualifications were useful. In Palestine, I had done a course on mines and explosives run by the Royal Engineers. I had trained with explosives again in the commandos, served in guerrilla-type operations in Abyssinia, operated against guerrillas in Palestine, and gained battle experience from fighting in Iraq, Syria, Persia, and the Western Desert. I had also been sent on a secret course in the grounds of the monastery at Emwas (the biblical Emmaus), where the students learnt about sabotage, mines, demolitions and guerrilla warfare before returning to pass on their skills to certain groups in their original units. These groups were earmarked to stay behind in Palestine should the Germans get that far; our forces would be withdrawn to Egypt while these stay-behind groups would hide in the mountains from where they would harry the Germans. It never happened, but a number of Jews and Arabs who had been on these courses used their knowledge later on against the British.

MO4 accepted me, but I had to stay with my regiment until summoned. My colonel received my application for a transfer sympathetically — possibly he was glad to be rid of a somewhat bolshie officer — and I did not rejoin my regiment until after the war.

On 1 January 1943, I reported to the HQ of MO4 in Rustem Buildings, Cairo. I was soon despatched on a month's course in Palestine to receive the standard training for agents in the field. The establishment was a requisitioned monastery on the top of Mount Carmel, with a superb view over Haifa and across the bay to Acre. I luckily avoided living in the very uncomfortable camp as an Arab friend, Roy Boutagy, had gone on holiday and had kindly lent me his luxurious flat adjoining the Windsor Annexe Hotel owned by his father. I was halfway up Mount Carmel and only five minutes' drive from the school.

There were thirty-six British students on the course, of whom only fifteen passed, and about fifty foreign students, mostly from the Balkans. The work was strenuous, starting at dawn with PT. We studied German and Italian weapons, uniforms, insignia, badges and organization, map-reading, explosives and demolitions, as well as such unorthodox subjects as sabotage of all types, the use of secret inks, tapping telephone lines, lockpicking and safe-blowing.

One lesson sticks in my memory. We were being shown the working of a time pencil attached to an incendiary device when it exploded prematurely, setting our classroom ablaze. The wooden hut was burning furiously, and our anxious instructor urged his pupils to fetch water and sand. One of our more cynical students commented, 'Let it burn down, and with no classroom we will get a half-holiday this afternoon'; and he was right.

On another occasion, a fellow student and I had to row out in the middle of the night in a small rubber dinghy to stick a limpet mine onto the wreck of the *Patria*, an illegal Jewish immigrant ship that had been lying drunkenly on its side in Haifa harbour for most of the war. It was pouring with rain, and we were soaked through but were prudent enough to be carrying flasks of whisky. The boat nearly upset as we completed our mission.

One instructor was a particular favourite. Stas Lazarowicz was a Polish officer who taught us the use of foreign weapons, as well as pistol shooting. A most charming and entertaining man, blind in one eye, he spoke a droll pidgin English and had a fine sense of humour. However, his cheerful manner hid a personal tragedy, for he had left Poland without knowing the fate of his family, and he had a bitter hatred for both the Germans and the Russians.

A short time after our course had ended, a spectacular raid was launched against our training school. The entire contents of the armoury, including over thirty machine guns, were stolen. Two military three-ton lorries containing men in uniform were allowed to drive into the camp by the Jewish security guards. Having broken into the armoury and loaded the contents onto the two lorries, they drove off, taking not only the guards but also the security officer, who was himself a Jew. It later transpired that all were members of the Jewish Agency, and the stolen weapons were no doubt used later by the Jewish underground army fighting the British; the unfortunate commandant had to face a court-martial.

Those of us who passed the course in Haifa were sent to a camp at Kabrit — one of many on the Suez Canal. It was the base for David Stirling's newly formed Special Air Service, famous later as the SAS, and it was here that they did their parachute training. SOE shared their training facilities, but we managed to avoid the intensive PT which the instructor maintained was necessary before making a jump. However, we learnt the essentials, which included jumping off the back of a truck going at 40 mph, and completed our six jumps in under a week.

Our first jumps were out of a Lockheed Hudson aircraft, which had a miserably small door in the side of the fuselage; moreover, its slowest speed was about 120 mph, too fast for a comfortable exit. Of the four jumps out of this aircraft, at heights starting at 1000 feet and getting down to 500 feet, I found the second the most frightening. At the first jump, one was fairly ignorant as to what to expect, and after the initial relief that the parachute had really opened — we carried no spare parachutes in those days — I found the descent exhilarating and enjoyable, but this feeling faded as one neared the ground, which we hit pretty hard; the impact, we were told, was like jumping off a twenty-foot wall.

Our last two jumps were at night out of a Dakota, which had a bigger door but less speed. We were then considered trained parachutists, entitled to two shillings a day extra pay and the right to wear the parachutist's badge. For security reasons, SOE men did not wear the badge until they were in the field, but as soon as we arrived we lost no time in having them sewn on. Copying a system started by David Stirling, we wore our badges on our breasts to indicate that we had done an operational jump — rather like getting one's first eleven colours at school. This privilege was very unpopular with the regular parachute troops, who were allowed to wear their badges only on their arms.

After the parachute course I was granted ten days leave, which I spent with my brother John at Asmara, in Eritrea, hitchhiking there and back from Cairo with the RAF. On the return journey, fate was on my side. The Dakota in which I was getting a lift had reached the end of the runway before take-off, when it was recalled by the control tower. To my fury a brigadier pulled his rank on me, saying he had priority, and I was turfed off. I left in another plane a few hours later. Near the end of the journey, the Dakota came down very low and we were all asked to keep a lookout as the aircraft ahead of us was overdue; we did not spot it, but the next day it was found to have crashed in the desert outside Cairo and there were no survivors.

Chapter II: Briefing in Cairo

The Special Operations Executive (SOE) was formed at Churchill's instigation. Its main role, to use his words to Hugh Dalton, the first Minister of Economic Warfare, was 'to set Europe ablaze'. Its tasks were to foster a spirit of resistance to the Germans in the occupied countries and then to set up resistance movements to act as a 'fifth column' when the time came for the Allies to invade.

After my dirty tricks course on Mount Carmel and my Eritrean interlude, I spent the next six weeks in Cairo at the HQ of MO4, then the cover name for the Middle East branch of SOE, which came under the Minister of Economic Warfare in London. MO4 switched names several times, becoming Force 133, Force 266, and Force 399.

In the Balkans, there was another reason for encouraging resistance. By the end of 1942, the war had reached a turning point. In October, the battle of Alamein started Rommel's retreat in the Western Desert, and in November the Russian counterattack at Stalingrad ended with the German surrender in February 1943. The Germans were now on the defensive.

Although they still occupied the whole of Europe, except Switzerland, Sweden and the United Kingdom, they knew that sooner or later the Allies would invade the European mainland, but of course they did not know when or where. They badly needed reinforcements in Russia and more troops in the north of France, where they expected the invasion.

They had a great number of garrison troops in the Balkans — about thirty divisions, or nearly half a million men. If the resistance movements could make themselves a thorough nuisance by guerrilla warfare and sabotage, these divisions would be tied down without being transferred to Russia or France.

The HQ of MO4 was in a block of requisitioned flats in a residential district of Cairo called Rustem Buildings. The current joke was that on telling an Egyptian taxi driver to go there, he would usually reply 'Yes, sah, to the headquarters of the British Secret Service.'

I spent the mornings in the office with McLean, being briefed for our impending drop, which we were told would be into Yugoslavia. I kept fit by bathing or playing tennis at the Gezira Club, and I also kept up my pistol practice under two instructors with reputations as crack shots. One was a British officer, Captain Grant Taylor, who had a pair of pearl-handled Colts with which he could literally hit the Ace of Spades at thirty yards range. The other was an American officer called Smith, whose claim to fame was that when in the FBI he had fired the shot that had killed the notorious gangster Dillinger.

The two officers mainly responsible for our briefing were Major Basil Davidson and Captain James Klugmann. Both were very helpful, but when our country of operations was changed to Albania, Davidson stopped briefing us, as he was involved in the Yugoslav section only. He later became a well-known writer of books and articles with left-wing views. Klugmann, who was in the administrative branch, continued to help us, even sending messages to my mother after I had reached Albania. I found him charming, though he was an acknowledged Communist. As Russia was our ally, nobody seemed to mind Communists in SOE HQ, but later in the war this did cause problems.

It was McLean who got us switched from Yugoslavia to Albania. He had worked out a plan based on sketchy information, and Brigadier Keeble, then head of MO4, gave his approval.

MO4 was divided into country sections. The Albanian section then consisted of one person — only Mrs Margaret Hasluck. She was an elderly lady, the widow of a famous archaeologist, with greying hair swept back into a bun and a pink complexion with bright blue eyes; she reminded me of an old-fashioned English nanny. Full of energy and enthusiasm, she was totally dedicated to her beloved Albania. She had lived for about twenty years in her home near Elbasan, studying Albanian anthropology and folklore, on which she was one of the greatest authorities. Her closest Albanian friend was Lef Nosi, a distinguished and patriotic figure who had taken a prominent part in the creation of an independent Albania after the First World War.

In 1939, the Italians expelled Mrs Hasluck from Albania as a spy, which at that time she was not, but when she moved to Turkey she was recruited by British Intelligence. For the next two years she worked there, collecting every scrap of information on Albania, keeping in touch with Albanians both in and out of the country, until finally she was brought to Cairo to set up the Albanian section in the SOE HQ.

I knew nothing about Albania, but I gleaned from reference books that it was a small country not much bigger than Wales; bounded on the west by the Adriatic, in the north and east by Yugoslavia, and in the south by Greece. It was dominated by mountains running mainly north and south, with rivers running down to a coastal plain and into the sea. The population was estimated at about a million. Of these, some 800,000 were Moslems — divided equally into Sunnis and Bektashis. There were 120,000 Roman Catholics, mainly in the north, and 80,000 Orthodox in the south. Descended from the ancient

Illyrians, the Albanians are a distinct group of their own, but divided into two main tribes — the Ghegs in the north and the Tosks in the south.

For almost five hundred years, Albania was occupied and ruled by the Turks. But in 1912 the Turks were defeated by the Austro-Hungarians and their Balkan allies, and in 1913 Albania was declared an independent state. During World War I, however, Albania again fell under occupation, this time by the armies of the various belligerents, notably the French, who were fighting the Austrians. After the war, Albania was again freed from foreign domination and her 1913 frontiers restored. These were ratified in 1926, much to the disgust and opposition of the Albanians, for although a million of them lived within them, a further million lived outside. Of these, most were Moslems who lived in Kosovo, which had become a province of Yugoslavia; the minority lived elsewhere in Yugoslavia and in the Epirus area of northern Greece. The Albanian state claimed these areas but were rebuffed.

Independent Albania at once became caught in a tug-of-war for influence between Italy and Yugoslavia — both for strategic and commercial reasons. Mussolini wanted to expand eastwards, and Albania had important chrome mines and oil fields. Both countries vied in cultivating the tribal chiefs, who, since the war, had either fought each other or intrigued for power. By 1924 Ahmed Bey Zog, a Gheg chieftain from the Mati area, had emerged as the clear leader and became Prime Minister. However, he was driven out of the country by the opposition party of Mgr Fan Noli and fled to Yugoslavia. There he raised an army of Kosovars and, with the connivance of the Yugoslav government, marched into Albania and occupied Tirana, the capital, deposing the government of Fan Noli.

In 1925 he invited Colonel Frank Stirling, who had been asked by the Albanian government in 1923 to become Adviser to the Minister of the Interior, to take on the additional duty of Inspector General of Gendarmerie, authorizing him to engage nine British officers as sub-inspectors. They became servants of the Albanian government; the British government was in no way involved, although it was happy to see Italian influence eroded.

Political reasons were behind Zog's choosing British officers for the gendarmerie; it would have upset the Yugoslavs if he had employed Italians, as he already had Italian instructors in the Albanian army. After a year, Colonel Stirling resigned and was succeeded by Major General Sir Jocelyn Percy, a distinguished officer from World War I, who commanded eight British officers and some three thousand gendarmes.

Though originally supported by the Yugoslavs, Zog gradually became more subject to Italian influence. In 1928 he was proclaimed King of the Albanians, having been elected their first President in 1925. In spite of Italian pressure to remove them he kept on the British gendarmerie officers under Percy, until he finally yielded to Italian pressure in 1938 and was forced to terminate their contracts. However, Mussolini was increasingly irritated by Zog's independence, and on Good Friday 1939 Italy invaded Albania.

In spite of some resistance, notably by a gendarme officer named Major Abas Kupi in the defence of Durazzo, the stronger Italian army quickly overran the country, and King Zog and his beautiful wife Queen Geraldine were forced to flee into Greece with their son Leka, who was only a few days old. The family spent the rest of the war in England.

In our Cairo briefing, the Italians in Albania were reckoned at six divisions, including one of Alpini, but no Germans had yet appeared. Although there was an Italian-sponsored government, the loyalty of the Albanian army and gendarmerie to the Italians was unknown.

Mrs Hasluck was convinced that the Albanians would do all that they could to drive the Italians out. She had already received reports of guerrilla bands in the mountains and of an organization said to co-ordinate their activities, but no one knew whether it really existed, who supported it, and who controlled it. The only leaders' names of whom she had heard were Abas Kupi, Baba Faja, Myslim Pesa, and Muharrem Bajraktari. With this scanty information, McLean and I were to be sent to Albania to contact any of these supposed bands and to find out what help they needed against their Italian occupiers. We could carry with us *laissez-passers* urging Albanians to help us, signed by General Percy and Mrs Hasluck.

On most mornings, Mrs Hasluck taught us all she could about the country and its customs and language. Based on the ancient Illyrian, but borrowing words from the Roman and Turkish occupations, Albanian is a difficult language with a Roman script. I was stumped by the complicated grammar but picked up some useful words and phrases.

We decided against doing a 'blind' drop — one with no previous contact on the ground — for we knew nobody in Albania, and there were no British officers or agents there. There was, however, a British Mission in the mountains of northern Epirus in Greece, so it was arranged for us to drop to a reception committee there. From Epirus we would walk into Albania and build up our contacts afresh.

The groups known as British Missions that were dropped into the Balkans normally consisted of a leader or head of mission, an expert in explosives and demolitions, a wireless operator, and an interpreter, who was often a national of the country concerned. Our team was to be five strong: I was to be second-in-command with the rank of captain to Billy McLean who, as head of the mission, was promoted Major.

Two years younger than myself, McLean had been at Eton and Sandhurst, before joining the Royal Scots Greys as a regular officer in 1939. In Abyssinia, around Gondar, he had led in action several thousand Abyssinian irregulars, as well as a battalion of Eritreans, reorganized at the 79th (McLean's) Foot, and had won a fine reputation as a guerrilla leader. He was tall and slim, with long straight hair that he had a habit of sweeping back as it fell over his eyes. His charming character seemed languid and nonchalant to the point of idleness, but underneath this facade he was brave, physically tough and extremely intelligent, with a quick and active mind. Very attractive to, and fond of, women, his attitude seemed governed by the principle of safety in numbers. As cavalry officers we both had much in common, but whereas his interests lay chiefly in people and politics, mine lay more in the material aspects of life.

The third member of our mission was Garry Duffy, a lieutenant in the Royal Engineers, and an expert in mines and demolitions. Dark and slight with a small moustache, he had a fine contempt for all foreigners. He had no love for Greeks or Albanians, or for their food or their habits, but he was a brave and resourceful officer who proved his value on the spot.

Corporal Williamson, a short, dark, freckled Scotsman from the Black Watch, was a wireless operator with an infinite capacity for long hours of hard work, whose sense of humour emerged at its highest as conditions became more difficult; in short, he was a typical 'Jock'.

Finally, there was Elmaz — small and thickset, with black close-cropped hair and brown eyes, and the flat back to his head that was a typical feature of many Albanians. His English was only fair, and though he never showed much enthusiasm for coming he reluctantly agreed to do so; he had been very difficult from the beginning because he wanted to discuss his future mission with various Albanian friends in Egypt, which for security reasons was forbidden.

Before leaving we had a short course in escaping from Captain Jasper Maskelyne, a famous magician in peacetime. Various items such as magnetic fly-buttons, mini-compasses concealed in buttons, pencil clips that pointed north when balanced on the tip of the pencil, files, silk maps, and money were sewn into our clothes; we then drew our full kit which included not only weapons and special clothing but also gold, issued in thousand-sovereign bags.

We left Cairo after a series of farewell parties and on 11 April 1943, my twenty-seventh birthday, we arrived by train at Derna, from where we were driven to a bleak camp on the edge of the airfield some miles from the town. For security reasons we were confined to the camp like prisoners, so we hoped our stay would be short. On the airfield was a squadron of Halifax bombers under the command of Squadron Leader Jimmy Blackburn, who was famous for his skill and accuracy in dropping agents and supplies into enemy-held territory.

There were about a dozen officers in the camp, mostly Greek and Yugoslav, with a few British, all anxiously waiting to be dropped into the Balkans. Weather and lack of aircraft often caused delay, but it was even more depressing when missions flew over their areas but had to return without finding their dropping zones. To celebrate a departure, we drank a good deal in the bar to use up our remaining Egyptian currency. It was an anti-climax when those to whom we had bidden a noisy farewell the night before turned up for breakfast next morning.

Our mission had a setback the day before we left; just as we were trying on our parachutes, Elmaz suddenly refused to come unless he could first communicate with various Albanians in Cairo. There were no communications from Derna that he could use, and anyway it was too late; however, no persuasion by McLean could make him change his mind, so we handed him over to the security officer. Much later I learnt that he had been sent to a camp in the Sudan, where he spent the rest of the war. His loss was a blow, but we could not afford further delay, so we decided to drop without an interpreter, hoping to find someone suitable once we got there.

Chapter III: Drop into Greece and move to the Albanian frontier

Five long days after arriving in Derna we drove out to the Halifax in the late afternoon, comforted by the fact that Jimmy Blackburn was to be our pilot. That afternoon, we had supervised the packing of our kit into small cylindrical metal canisters, three of which fitted into a container about six-foot-long with a parachute packed at one end, and had watched them being slung on the bomb racks. We were already dressed for the drop; over our battledress we wore flying suits, and over this we wore padded overalls which did up with a complicated system of zips. By the time we had our parachute harnesses on, we felt like trussed chickens. As we approached the big Halifax bombers, they looked like prehistoric monsters in the evening light.

Soon we were flying north, out to sea, steadily climbing as the coast of Africa receded in the evening light. It began to get very cold and the sky became darker, but after the windows had been blacked out and the lights turned on we felt more comfortable.

My feelings were a mixture of excitement and fear, and though the rest of the party slept I couldn't. I had brought the latest *Horse and Hound* and *Tatler* for the journey, and I read every detail including the advertisements.

After two and a half hours we approached the coast of Greece, and our dispatcher, an RAF sergeant, told us it was time to put on our parachutes. He added that on this part of the journey, we might meet enemy fighters or 'flak'. Luckily, we met neither. After checking that the static lines from our parachutes were securely fastened to the bars in the fuselage, the dispatcher opened a large circular trapdoor in the floor. The wind and the engines roared, and I shivered as we took up our positions on the edge of the hole, with our legs dangling down into space. My mind was diverted from the thought of the drop by the fascination of peering down at the lights of the Greek villages and the snow on the mountains below, and for a moment I forgot the butterflies in my stomach.

At last we saw our recognition signals — nine fires forming the letter 'V' — and the aircraft began to circle and lose height. Then the red warning light in the roof went on and the dispatcher shouted, 'Action Stations!'. After a quick, reassuring tug at my static line and a glance at my companions' faces, I slid my behind nearer the edge of the hole, firmly gripping the side. A few seconds later the engines throttled back, the light changed to green, and the dispatcher shouted 'Go!', at the same time hitting McLean on the back. He pushed himself forward and dropped down the hole into space, followed almost immediately by me, then by Williamson and Duffy. As this was our first parachute jump out of a hole in the floor — even on dummies, we had practised out of side doors — it was surprising that our exits were made without mishap. People often broke their noses jumping out of Halifaxes by hitting them on the opposite side of the hole.

We dropped from two or three thousand feet. My first reaction was relief as my parachute billowed open. Our descent took barely a couple of minutes, the noise of the Halifax engines fading as the aircraft gradually disappeared from view up the valley, below the tops of the snow-capped mountains; then came a silence broken only by the whistling of the wind in my rigging lines. I found myself drifting close to McLean, and, thinking I might overtake him and hit his parachute, I shouted a warning, but luckily we did not collide. As we neared the ground, I heard the jingling of the bells of the goats or sheep in their herds, then shouts, followed by a heavy thud as I hit the Epirote mountains of Greece.

I made a bad landing, tearing a muscle in my leg, which was scarcely surprising, since our dropping zone[1] was a dried-up riverbed of stones and rocks. I landed only five yards from one of the signal fires, which spoke very highly of Jimmy Blackburn's skill. I had barely time to hit the buckle releasing my parachute when a large figure bore down on me, wearing battledress festooned with bandoliers and sporting a huge beard. I was still struggling to disentangle myself when he seized me, dragged me to my feet and kissed me on both cheeks, murmuring words that were indeed Greek to me. After much handshaking and shouting, he produced a bottle from his pocket and urged me to drink; this I was only too willing to do, for my mouth was very dry. I did not much like the taste of the stuff; it turned out to be ouzo, which I later grew to like.

Within a few minutes we all gathered near one of the fires, the others having landed without incident; the Halifax made another couple of runs dropping our stores, then flew over us very low while we gave the signal on a torch to indicate that we had all landed safely. Then our last physical link with the friendly world outside headed off towards its base in Africa.

As soon as the aeroplane had disappeared we met Captain John Cook, the British officer in charge of the reception party. He told us that his group contained some fifty guerrillas, known as *andartes*. They wore British battledress and bandoliers and carried a variety of weapons ranging from knives and pistols to rifles and tommy guns. They were clearly an expert reception committee, for they were already obliterating all the

---

[1] Often referred to as 'DZ'.

signs of the fires when the Halifax disappeared. I was somewhat alarmed at first by all the shouting and singing that went on in an area I imagined to be occupied by Germans and Italians, but the nearest enemy garrison was at Ioannina (Yannena), some twelve miles away as the crow flew, and at least eighteen hours' march over mountain tracks.

Our stores were quickly collected. Two parachutes had failed to open, one with our wireless set. One case of ammunition was never found, but Cook told us that this was not unusual — ammunition was very highly prized by the *andartes*, and on most drops a box or two tended to disappear. Otherwise the drop was a success.

All the stores were quickly loaded onto mules, and we set off up a steep track that wound up the side of the valley. McLean went with Cook in a different direction to meet a Brigadier Myers, who was holding a conference the next day at the monastery of Romanon, about an hour and a half away.

After two hours climbing, with my leg hurting badly, we reached a small farmstead perched on the side of a very steep mountain. Dogs barked as we approached, and in the moonlight we could make out stone buildings with red-tiled roofs. Vines crept up the side of the houses and a few chinks of light showed through the wooden shutters over the glassless windows. The moonlit river glinted in the valley below. Above us, the snow-topped mountains looked grim and forbidding. Duffy, Williamson and I were warmly greeted by an Orthodox priest, wearing a black cassock and the customary black stovepipe hat. He was our host for the night.

Hospitable people were milling around, as well as our *andarte* escort. They took off our boots, fed us, gave us plenty of wine, and finally tucked us up for the night on mattresses laid on the floor. None of us understood a word they spoke, but we gathered that 'kala' meant 'good'.

We all fell asleep very quickly, tired out by the mental as well as the physical strain. We had left Derna in the evening, dropped shortly after midnight, climbed for over two hours, and now it was well after three in the morning. It was comforting to know that we were sheltered in a friendly house, and well filled with food and wine into the bargain.

The next morning, we loaded our stores on to the mules and walked for about an hour and a half to join McLean at Romanon monastery, the HQ of the British Mission led by Major Guy Micklethwait, who had previously served with McLean in Abyssinia.

It was a most exhilarating walk in the crisp air. The green mountains studded with large beech woods and with snow on the upper slopes made a lovely contrast with the blue sky and the green waters of the river in the valley below. Although I missed my friends in Cairo, I had no regrets in changing the Egyptian scene for one like this.

On arrival at Romanon, McLean met us in the courtyard of the monastery and led me upstairs to a room in which a British officer was seated at a refectory table reading some papers. He wore a blue forage cap, and the pips on his battledress proclaimed him a brigadier, and on his breast bore the ribbon of the DSO under parachute wings. Eddie Myers was then the senior British officer in Greece. A regular Sapper officer, he had led the famous action the previous November when Greek guerrillas, assisted by British officers, notably Colonel Monty Woodhouse, had destroyed the Gorgopotamos viaduct. Since then, he had been trying with little success to fix up a working agreement between the rival Greek political parties, to make them co-operate against the Italians and Germans rather than fight each other. He briefed us on all this before we moved on.

At this time, there were two major political parties in the field; the right wing, loyal to the King and the government in exile, known by the initials EDES and commanded by General Zervas, and the left wing, under strong Communist influence, known by the initials EAM and commanded locally by a Colonel Sarafis. A number of subsidiary political factions also had various initials, and it was at first confusing to discover who was on what side. In general, the right-wing guerrillas were called *andartes* and most of them sported beards, while the left wing referred to themselves as partisans and occasionally shaved. However, whatever their politics, it was still possible for British officers to serve as liaison officers with both of them. A civil war had not yet started, but it was only a matter of time.

We spent three nights at Romanon, sorting out our stores and re-packing them into mule loads. Williamson signalled Cairo, on Micklethwait's set, that ours was smashed and asked for an urgent replacement. My leg, too, had a chance to improve, for the local doctor who saw it recommended massage. The wife of one of the Greek officers at the HQ, a trained nurse, obliged.

We were keen not to waste time, so McLean decided that we would press on towards Albania and leave Williamson behind us to bring on the new set when we had set up a base. McLean, Duffy and I set off with a party shepherded by Cook with an escort of *andartes*, guides, mulemen, and ten mules carrying our stores.

Our first march lasted nine hours — which I found far too long — over winding mountain tracks. When we reached our stopping place for the night, a village school, the locals did not seem at all pleased to see us and were almost hostile. It turned out that they had been bombed by the Italians a few days before as a reprisal for harbouring guerrillas, so they were understandably rather frightened and jittery. That did not deter them from charging us an exorbitant sum for the sheep they sold us for our party's dinner.

We set off the next morning with fresh mules and mulemen, including two riding mules for McLean and me. They had the same wooden saddles as the pack mules, and the only comfortable way to ride was side-saddle. As our *andartes* were from EDES, they refused to escort us into Mospina, the village we were approaching, for it was in ELAS[2] hands. They said we would get a friendly reception if we went in alone, but neither McLean nor I liked the idea, for we had already heard of British officers being murdered for their gold during a handover like this. A friend of mine was murdered for his gold in Bulgaria.

Two or three British officers could easily disappear without the culprits being brought to book. The escort merely had to shoot us, collect our sovereigns, and report that they had already handed us over to their rivals, whom they could then blame. However, there was no alternative but to go on alone. So, after saying goodbye and thank you to our escort, McLean and I entered the village, leaving Duffy and the mule party some distance behind. To our relief, the ELAS men who met us on the outskirts of the village were expecting us and gave us a warm welcome.

After a meal we went on with fresh mules, for we had to cross the Yannena-Igoumenitsa road by night as it was patrolled by the Italians. Here we discovered that 'the road', which was referred to with bated breath, inspired great

---

[2] The military wing of EAM.

nervousness among the partisans. The actual crossing of the road was a military operation that our erstwhile instructors would not have been pleased to witness. The nearer we approached the road the more nervous our guides and escort became, until finally the whole column ground to a halt and refused to move. After a hurried conference McLean and I decided to lead the party across, and in due course we found ourselves quite alone on the road. Suddenly we were challenged in Greek, which neither of us understood, so we drew our pistols and lay flat on our faces without replying. Happily, a few moments later some of our escort arrived and answered. Our challengers were an ELAS patrol that had been sent out to meet us from Raikon, the next village, and escort us on our way. Because one of the guides lost the way, we did not reach Raikon until about three in the morning. We got used to guides losing the way, but on this first occasion we were very exasperated. Before going off to sleep, McLean and I discussed the events of the day and decided not to risk being killed by acting as advance guards to the men who were supposed to be guarding us.

We spent the night in another village school. These were often put at our disposal because we were a big party and a village house could not accommodate all of us; furthermore, individuals might lay themselves open to reprisals if they put us up in their own houses. Schools had been closed since the start of the war in Greece, for families needed their children to work either at home, in the fields, or as shepherds.

On we went the next day with a very helpful and entertaining Major Bocharis in charge of our escort. Before nightfall, he took us to a position from where we had a good view of the main road, where we watched a convoy of seven heavy lorries heading towards Yannena escorted by an armoured car. This whetted our appetites. They presented a very easy target for an ambush.

As soon as it was dark, we moved on. One of the mules put its foot in a hole and fell heavily; when it got up it had clearly broken its leg, the bone breaking through the skin. It stood there miserably on three legs while the muleman started to thrash it. I stopped him, drew my pistol and indicated that I was going to shoot it, whereupon all the mulemen took great exception and started shouting at me. McLean came back to see what all the row was about and found me losing my temper with the mulemen. Calming me, he reasoned that it was most unwise to have a scene with the locals, on whom so much depended, so I had to give in and the wretched animal carried on with only three legs. I learned that if a horse or mule broke a leg, it was the normal custom to put it in splints for a month while the animal did only light work, and that within six weeks it would be doing normal work again — which accounted for the number of mules we saw at work with very deformed legs. In time, one got inured to the appalling treatment meted out to animals in the Balkans and the Middle East.

We arrived at Kouklia village school before dawn for a few hours much needed sleep before we set off again, crossing the main Yannena to Gjirokastër road at midnight. Again, our escort became nervous near the road, but we reached the village of Vissani without incident. Despite the late hour we had our best reception to date, and we were given an excellent meal washed down with plenty of wine followed by ouzo. We slept it off in the local magistrate's courts.

They looked after us magnificently in Vissani. The villagers were celebrating Easter Day and there was an air of festivity, the girls looking very attractive in their colourful traditional dresses, and the men all wearing their Sunday best. We were given a number of coloured eggs, most of them stained scarlet; the small boys were playing a game with them in which they knocked each other's eggs together, and the one who cracked the other was the winner, rather like conkers.

We left the next day to a splendid send-off by the villagers, who lined the streets waving Greek flags, clapping and showering us with flowers. They clearly regarded us as liberators; I felt somewhat bogus because not only was liberation a long way off, but our aim was to reach Albania and help the Albanians, for whom the Greeks had little love.

After a seven-hour march we reached Drymades, the last village in Greece before the Albanian frontier, some hundred yards further on. At last Albania was in sight. We planned to stay here until we had made contact with the Albanian guerrillas, some of whom were said to be active on their side of the frontier, and with whom the Greek ELAS forces were in touch. Prospects looked good that evening: two Albanian partisans were produced, and we gave them a note asking to meet their leaders.

During the three days that we waited for an answer we explored the village, lazed in the sun and carried out various make-and-mend jobs. I wrote up my diary, which I was determined to keep though it was against wartime regulations.

Drymades was a very peaceful village on the eastern slopes of a large valley, with a range of craggy mountains towering on either side running north into Albania and south into Greece. The village had about fifty slate-roofed stone houses, mostly single-storey though the more prosperous had two floors. The villagers were poor, often short of essentials such as flour, maize, olive oil and sugar, yet they were extremely hospitable.

We were given two rooms in a house belonging to a man who spoke a little English. His teenage daughter did various household chores for us. She was a first-class seamstress who not only repaired our clothes, but made shirts and pyjamas out of my parachute, which I had managed to retain in spite of the attempts of certain light-fingered folk at Romanon to pinch it. At this stage of the war, parachutes were made of real silk and were of various colours — mine was pale blue. Later they were made of nylon, usually camouflage green, and those for stores were merely cotton.

Our party consisted of McLean, Duffy and me; but Cook, who had left us earlier, now rejoined us with a Captain Niko of the EAM and a character known as Black George, an Arab from Aden who had enlisted in the Palestine Pioneer Corps, and he claimed to be a corporal. Taken prisoner by the Germans when the British evacuated Greece, he had escaped and had been about two years in the mountains where he learnt Greek and attached himself to a British Mission. He was now with Cook, but we accepted his request to stay with us. He was a most useful member of the party: he could interpret for us, bargain with the locals, deal with the mulemen, and perform endless other jobs. He was known as Black George, not only for his dark complexion, but to distinguish him from another George, a fair-haired Greek boy who was one of the partisans attached to our entourage, whom we called Greek George. Black George was a likeable rogue, and we had no doubt he was making a very good profit out of his job.

Our food was much the same for the first few months. When the mission was static we had three meals a day — breakfast, lunch, and supper. Lunch and supper were preceded by appetizers known as *meze* washed down by ouzo in Greece and raki in Albania. Breakfast consisted of excellent yoghurt from sheep's milk, eggs, unappetizing bread made from maize flour, butter and cheese, usually from goat or sheep, and tea from our own supplies. For lunch we had eggs or meat — goat, mutton or chicken — potatoes or rice, and tinned fruit from our own supplies, if we had any. As the meat was always boiled so much it was completely tasteless, we used to add our own curry powder. We usually drank the local wine with lunch. We had no tea meal, and supper normally started with a thick soup to which beans or rice had been added, followed by eggs or meat — again curried — with salad made with olive oil with a generous sprinkling of onions or garlic, finishing off with bread and cheese. We drank ouzo both before and after supper and wine with the meal, sometimes followed by a form of raw brandy known as *tsipouro*.

While McLean and I made every effort to enjoy the local food, which actually we did, we could never get Duffy to do so. He was always saying, 'I can't eat this muck', and 'Oh! for a steak and kidney pie, or roast beef and Yorkshire pudding.'

The attitude of the Greek peasants towards their women was very similar to that of the Egyptians. For most of the day, the men sat in the *kaphencia* (local coffee shops-cum-bars) drinking coffee, playing backgammon, and talking politics, only going home at mealtimes; the women would be working hard either in the home or in the fields. When travelling, the man would invariably be riding a donkey or mule in front, while the woman brought up the rear, staggering under a load of baggage.

At the end of the third day in Drymades, word came that we could move into Albania, so we set off next morning, leaving Cook to return to his base after seeing us out of his area. After a short walk we passed a derelict stone hut, which had been the customs house and frontier guard-post: the actual frontier between Greece and Albania. Now that we were on Albanian soil, we had achieved the first step of our mission. The next stage — getting in touch with Albanian guerrillas and encouraging them to fight the common enemy — was not to prove so easy.

Chapter IV: First partisan contacts and action

We arrived at the Albanian village of Sopiç in time for a satisfying lunch of bean soup, mutton — both hot and an improvement on the cold and congealed food in Greece — and yoghurt, accompanied by local red wine. We dossed down in a better class of house than we had stayed in in Greece. It was the current Italian policy to treat the Albanians better than the Greeks, with the result that they had more privileges and better food supplies.

In Sopiç we met a man who had emigrated to the United States, worked there until he had made enough money on which to retire, and then returned to his native village to spend the rest of his days. He could barely understand English, and what little he spoke was with such a broad American accent that it was often unintelligible. We later met many men of this type, and they produced American passports with great pride; sadly, their stay in America had improved neither their characters nor their morals, and we found that their contact with the West had made the majority both avaricious and dishonest.

On our first evening, everyone gathered in the village tavern to listen to the BBC news in Greek. It was most heartening to see what a good effect it had on their morale, and to be told that they considered the BBC news reported the truth, while they regarded the German and Italian news as lies and propaganda. Later in the war, certain foreign sections of the BBC became influenced by Communist sympathizers or fellow travellers, and when the news had a Communist bias it caused much embarrassment to those British Liaison Officers[3] attached to the various anti-Communist resistance movements, and their work was greatly handicapped, as I know from personal experience.

Most of the inhabitants of Sopiç spoke only Greek, though some spoke Albanian as well. A few told us in confidence, but would not say so in public, that they would prefer to be under Greek, rather than Albanian, rule. During our travels in the Greek/Albanian frontier areas, we frequently encountered this problem. Both Greece and Albania had claims on each other's territory, based on the ethnic population. The Greek claim that the Greek Orthodox population of Southern Albania desired union with Greece did not appear to be true, and only a minority of Greek-speaking villages desired union with Greece. At that time in 1943, only a very few Albanian-speaking villages on the Greek side of the border wanted union with Albania; but after the civil war that raged in those areas in 1945, the population and their views may well have changed.

We moved the next day, spending the night in the small village of Skorë, and arrived at Poliçan in time for a lunch that was memorable for the liberal supply of champagne served with it. After discussion with the village leaders, we were advised that it was not safe to proceed further north with our very conspicuous column of mules. In Communist areas, most villages had a small committee of leaders, usually comprising the schoolmaster, the priest, and a man who we assumed was the commissar. We decided that Duffy and Black George should return to Sopiç with the mules while McLean and I continued north.

We set out in the pouring rain, and violent thunderstorms continued all the morning. I arrived at Shepër, the next village

---

[3] BLOs.

on our route, soaked to the skin in spite of my new army mackintosh, which leaked badly. At this stage of the war, the British army was not yet equipped with any garment capable of keeping out the rain, for gas capes and groundsheets were inadequate to keep a soldier dry. I had some sympathy with the Chinese army, who were alleged to carry umbrellas into battle, and I wished I had my London umbrella with me.

At Shepër we heard that the partisan leader we were hoping to contact was in the next village, Nivan, so we pressed on and arrived there that night, staying in the house of a man who had owned a restaurant in America. He not only gave us an excellent dinner, but also produced real beds for us in place of the customary mattresses on the floor. Nivan was the first village we had entered which was completely Albania, for Skorë was entirely Greek-speaking, and Poliçan half Greek and half Albanian. On arrival we were told that Bedri Spahiu, the local guerrilla leader, would be arriving the next day to meet us.

On the following morning, appropriately May 1st, he arrived accompanied by some of his *çeta*[4] — the name for a guerrilla band in Albanian. Mostly young men, they wore a mixture of military uniform and civilian clothes, usually with crossed bandoliers, and carried rifles. Their political views were evident, for their caps all sported a red star and they gave the Communist clenched-fist salute.

Bedri Spahiu was a dour character. He had been a regular officer in the Albanian army until he was imprisoned for being involved in a plot to overthrow King Zog. On release, he had been a motor salesman, in 1940 he had joined the Fascist Party, but a year later he had transferred his sympathies and joined the Albanian Communist Party.

---

[4] Ç in Albanian is pronounced 'ch' as in 'church'.

Our meeting was not the success we had hoped. We had naively assumed that he would welcome officers from a country at war with his enemies, who were prepared to help in fighting the Italian occupiers of his country. On the contrary, he gave the impression that he was suspicious, if not openly hostile, of our intentions, and bluntly informed us that we could not move any further into Albania but would be well advised to return to Greece at once. His reason for this, which he repeated several times, was that there had been 'une réaction fasciste' in the valley. As we spoke in French, this could have meant either that he was referring to Fascist reactionaries in the valley — bearing in mind that in Communist jargon anyone who is not a Communist is a Fascist — or else that the Italians had started a counterattack against the guerrillas in the valley.

However, the important point that emerged from our talks came when he informed us that he was a member of the 'Lëvizje Nacional Çlirimtare', known for short as the LNÇ, the Albanian for 'National Movement of Liberation'. This was our first contact with this organization, about which nothing definite was known; they had their headquarters, he told us, in the centre of the country, not far from Tirana. After some persuasion, he agreed to forward a letter from us to their HQ but added that it would take at least ten days to get a reply, and in the meantime he insisted we return to Greece to await it.

We had little option in the matter, so left for Drymades the next day. It had been a most disappointing start to our efforts to help the Albanians, but we put our hopes in the letter to the LNÇ HQ and could but patiently await their reply.

Our low spirits were revived in Poliçan, where we found a wedding in progress. We were immediately invited to join as guests by the father of the bride, who proudly informed us that he had been a sergeant in the Greek Royal Guard; to prove it, he showed us a photograph of himself in Evzone uniform. When I told him that I too was a 'Royal Guardsman', the drink flowed even stronger. After the ceremony, during which McLean and I followed the others in kissing first the priest, second the Bible, then the bride and finally the bridegroom, we went outside where a fusillade of shots rang out to express the guests' joy at this happy union. Leaving them all dancing in the street to the sounds of a fiddle and a flute, for we had politely refused to join in this part of the proceedings, we staggered off on the next stage of our journey. At Sopiç we found that Duffy had been joined by Williamson, who had brought the new wireless set that had been dropped to him after we had left him behind at Romanon.

The next morning Williamson made contact with Cairo, and our morale improved with the thought that from now on we should have a link with our friends in the outside world.

We made fresh plans. McLean and Williamson would remain at Drymades and await the reply from the LNÇ. Duffy could be usefully employed in doing a reconnaissance of the roads and bridges in the Gjirokastër area, which lay some distance to our west. I would return to Vissani and from there attempt to enter Albania in the area of Korçë (in Greek, Koritza), try to make contact with any guerrillas positioned there, and do a general reconnaissance of any roads, bridges and Italian troop concentrations that happened to be on the way.

I had no wireless set, but took two mules, one of which was to carry a load of 2000 sovereigns which we had taken in error from Micklethwait's mission, and which it had been arranged that I should hand over to Cook at Vissani. Even though they were contained in a small canvas bag, 1000 sovereigns were quite heavy, and we found 2000 was a reasonable load for a mule. I set off with two guides, and on coming to a very inviting stream I stripped off all my clothes and had a wash, followed by a refreshing bathe. The two guides were amazed, for the locals seldom stripped or washed thoroughly. Throughout our stay in Albania McLean and I conscientiously washed and shaved every morning, providing an entertaining spectacle in the villages, and frequently a crowd of villagers turned up to watch this unusual sight.

While waiting for Cook at Vissani, I was taken to visit the scene of a battle by a Greek officer who had fought in the campaign between the Greeks and Italians in 1940. The usual signs of debris and fighting were evident, including many trenches and graves. After Cook had arrived and I handed over the sovereigns, I took an EAM guide and crossed the Yannena-Leskovik road about five minutes before an Italian convoy, to the visible alarm of my mulemen. We then had to make an eight-hour detour on finding that a small stream that was usually fordable had turned into an impassable raging torrent. In both Greece and Albania, it was frequent for small streams, or even dried-up riverbeds, to become deep and broad rivers in a very short time after heavy rainfall in the mountains.

After two days' march we reached the town of Koritza; with over 3000 inhabitants, it was the largest town I had yet visited in Greece. As I was in uniform and the first British officer they had seen, they gave me an overwhelming reception, during which a large part of the town turned out. To my dismay I was asked to make a speech, and an impromptu one at that. Speeches have never been my strong point, so I was lucky in having an interpreter who took at least four times as long to interpret anything that I said, so at least I had time to think what I was going to say next. I urged my listeners to have patience, for the British Army would most certainly return to

Greece; in the meantime, I asked them to trust and help the British officers who had been sent to Greece to assist them in their struggle against the Italian and German occupiers of their country; I concluded by saying that victory for the Allies was only a matter of time, and was able to end my speech by using one of the very few words I had learnt in Greek — 'Kalliniki', meaning 'Victory'.

Some of their relief at seeing me was explained the next day, when I was made aware of the situation that existed in the town. My two EAM guides, or guards, never left my side, but large numbers of people would come up to shake my hand. On two occasions, a note was pressed into my palm without my two followers noticing. On getting back to my room I read these; both were written in English and said roughly the same. 'Did I realize that I was in the hands of ELAS? Did I know that they held power in the town by force and terror? Did I know that 90 per cent of the population were pro-Zervas?' One note further pressed me to visit a certain shop the next day on the pretext of making a purchase.

This I did, but as usual my two escorts went with me. Going into the shop I was greeted effusively by the owner in French, but when I quickly told him my escorts could understand French he tried his best, unsuccessfully, to get them to leave us. He then pressed me to stay for coffee, almost forcing me to sit down at his desk. When he brought the coffee, he offered me the tray, turned his back on the escorts and motioned me to look under the blotter where I saw a large envelope addressed to 'Mister English Captain'. I was able to slide this surreptitiously into my pocket as I drank the coffee and on returning to my room read the letter. It was signed by ten people and contained a long list of complaints against the

EAM and implored me to send for General Zervas's EDES forces to take the town over.

As my aim was to get into Albania as soon as I could, and not to become involved in Greek politics, the best I could do was to pass on the information later to Micklethwait, for Konitsa was in his area of operations.

That morning the EAM produced a man from Albania to whom I gave a letter to the *çeta* leader, whom I had been told was commanding a band operating in the Leskovik area. The following day brought news of his whereabouts, so, without waiting for a reply to my letter I slipped out of Konitsa in the middle of the night, not wishing the locals to see in which direction I was heading, and I then crossed the frontier into Albania for the second time.

Our track, passable only for mules, took a line roughly parallel to the main road in the valley but several hundred feet above it. I was able to see Italian traffic quite clearly, and at one point stopped to photograph a bridge, which was of sufficient importance for the Italians to have some twenty soldiers guarding it. Always a keen photographer, I found full scope for my hobby in Albania and, having a telescopic lens for my operational Leica camera, I made the most of every opportunity.

At a small village some hours' march further on, we found the *çeta*. The leader, Sulo Kozelli, had a band of thirty men, all with red stars in their hats, who greeted me with the clenched-fist salute and shouts of 'Vdekje Fashizmit' (Death to Fascism) to which I was expected to reply 'Liri Popullit' (Liberty to the People). This was the slogan used at every opportunity by the partisans such as, on greeting, as a toast when drinking, or on leave-taking. On remarking to my guide that I supposed all these people were, like him, Communists, he replied, 'No, not

Communists, democrats!' It appeared a well-equipped *çeta*, for as well as a rifle for every man, they had four Italian Breda light machine guns and one heavy machine gun.

Using as interpreters my guides, to whom I spoke in schoolboy French and who translated into what sounded like a mixture of Greek and Albanian, I had over two hours conversation with Sulo Kozelli. He was very forthcoming about the Italians, and I made notes of all the garrisons and posts as he indicated them to me on a map. When he told me that an action against the Italians was imminent, I asked him if I could be attached to his *çeta*. He seemed very unwilling to agree to this, and later I discovered he was not sure of my bona fides, suspecting that I had come to spy on behalf of the Greeks. However, when he told me that a representative of the LNÇ as well as the commandant of all the local *çeta* in the area were both coming to see him the next day, I persuaded him to take me with him to meet them.

The two escorts from the EAM left me and from then on two Albanian partisans were permanently attached to me, one of whom spoke fair French. I told Sulo Kozelli that I did not think they were necessary, but he replied that they were for my own safety. By now I realized that having an escort was an inconvenience that I would have to endure, for they never wanted me out of their sight. My contacts had to be with people of their own choosing, and these were naturally those with similar political views.

I asked Sulo Kozelli if I could make a close reconnaissance of Leskovik. He agreed. We descended to within half a mile of the town, and through my binoculars I could see details of the barracks, Italian transport, and soldiers walking about. I drew a sketch of the town and was then taken to lunch nearby with a truly eccentric character, Colonel Osman Gazepi. He was an old man who had formerly been a colonel in the Turkish army and claimed to be a close friend of King Zog. He said that he had contact with the Italians, for whom he professed an utter contempt, and was a staunch supporter of the LNÇ. This seemed unusual to me, for he came from a family of Beys, owned many hundreds of acres of vineyards, and was not the type I would have thought would have had much sympathy with the Communists, though his two daughters may well have. As I was taken to lunch with him by my two partisan escorts, I assumed that he had their approval, but during an excellent lunch of lamb and his home-grown wine, he gave the impression of being mentally deranged.

Returning to the *çeta* meant an all-night march. Crossing the Korçë-Leskovik road caused less panic than in Greece, and we reached a village in the early morning. I lay down on the floor of a room and slept soundly until the evening, when I was told that the *çeta* commandant had arrived and would see me. In another room I found a young man in Italian uniform, who introduced himself in French as Nexhip Vinçani. He said he was in a great hurry as his troops were about to attack Leskovik, so I asked if I could come with him. He agreed to let me watch the attack from a position on the hillside, but insisted that I should obey Sulo Kozelli's wishes, since the latter was responsible for my safety. After saying we would have a longer talk later, he abruptly left. Sulo Kozelli then said that if I was to watch the battle I must have a bigger bodyguard, so four new members were added to my original two, one of whom was a partisan girl; aged about twenty and no beauty, she was wearing trousers, and was armed with a rifle, bandolier and pistol.

Leskovik was said to be held by one battalion of Italian infantry, with attached troops such as engineers and supply troops; some further fifty *carabinieri* or gendarmerie were also stationed in the town. Nexhip Vinçani had told me that his aim was to drive the Italians out of the town and to capture all their arms, equipment and food, adding that the attack would start on the night of 15-16 May. I saw little of the start other than the flashes of grenades bursting and the lights of flares fired by the Italians.

The fighting lasted for twenty-four hours, during most of which I watched from a hill overlooking the town. During the day, I could both see and hear the mortar bombs fired by the partisans falling on and around the Italian barracks. Three Italian fighters circled over the town at frequent intervals dropping small bombs and machine-gunning the partisan positions in the town, and their din was added to the sound of rifle and machine gun fire on the ground. The exchange of fire between the partisans and the Italians seldom slackened, and, having been told that in World War I it took about twenty tons of lead to kill one man, I tried to guess what casualties would result from all this noise.

At the headquarters I was able to see the messengers coming in, very hot, breathless, and sweaty from their climb, shouting all their news in their excitement. From all accounts, in the morning the action was going well; thirty Italians were reported killed for the loss of two partisans, though I was a bit suspicious of these figures considering that the partisans were attacking and the Italians defending. There was no doubt, however, that the Italians had been confined to their barracks, while the partisans occupied the rest of the town; I was able to confirm this through my binoculars. One of the messengers said that the partisans had broken into the barrack area and pinned down the Italians in one small sector, but unfortunately this included the arms store and the magazine.

Three highly successful ambushes were mounted on the Italian columns which were trying to relieve the Leskovik garrison. Nexhip Vinçani had rightly foreseen that these columns would come from the nearest Italian units at Korçë, Përmet, and Yannena. The roads were blocked, and a strong group of partisans took up positions in the hills from which they could fire on any convoy halted by the roadblocks. I had a fine ringside seat of the ambush carried out on the Italian column from Korçë. As soon as the convoy rounded a bend, they were halted by a roadblock made from rocks and boulders rolled onto the road; a murderous fire was opened on them from all sides, and I could see the Italians leaping out of their lorries to try to take cover, and several were hit and fell. The partisans captured much equipment and four machine guns and thirteen prisoners, whom they shot out of hand.

In the afternoon, the three Italian fighters were joined by three Caproni bombers. From reports coming in, and from the behaviour of the partisans themselves, it was clear that the bombs had a very damaging effect on their morale, and finally Nexhip Vinçani ordered a withdrawal.

That night we left the area, marching fast along mule tracks in the mountains until we reached the village of Vithkuq. I vividly recall the clatter of the men and mules as they stumbled and kicked against the stones and rocks on the paths, the clanking of the equipment and the creaking of the saddles on the mules, the rattle of a man's rifle as it carelessly hit an overhanging rock or branch, and his muttered oath; in marked contrast was the sweet song of the nightingales, which abounded in Albania. Added to all this was the smell, usually a mixture of human and mule sweat blended with garlic, and the reek of locally grown tobacco.

On this particular march the partisans insisted that I should not be seen in my uniform, for they alleged that a number of Greek-speaking Albanians in the villages we passed were Italian informers. So I wore an old Italian army raincoat over my uniform and a partisan hat with a red star in it, and I was urged to give the Communist clenched fist salute to anyone we passed on the way or in the villages.

In retrospect, it is now obvious that the real object of this deception was to prevent my presence becoming known to any members of the rival organization, the Balli Kombëtar. The partisans had already told me that a *çeta* led by a certain Safet Butka had been active near Leskovik, and that they had been helping the Italians to fight the partisans; they were referred to as fascists, traitors and criminals. It later transpired that the band of Professor Safet Butka had been in the area, that he had known of my presence, and was very anxious to get in touch with me.

The Balli Kombëtar, which was also called the National Front, and whose members were either referred to as 'Ballists' or 'Nationalists', was certainly not what the partisans alleged it to be. It was a patriotic party of the more conservative elements, and their President was Mid'hat Frashëri, one of the architects of Albanian independence in 1913. Though most of them disliked the Greeks and Yugoslavs almost as much as the Italians, and therefore suspected British motives, they had not collaborated with the Italians. On the other hand, their intense hatred of Communism made them bitter enemies of the partisans, and armed clashes between their rival *çetas* had already occurred. They too, like the partisans, had their slogan, and greeted each other with 'Shqipëria Shqiptarëvet' (Albania for the Albanians) to which the reply was 'Vedkje Tradhetarëvet' (Death to Traitors).[5]

When we got to Vithkuq I was escorted into a small room with only a slit in the wall for ventilation, through which shone a beam of light. I was informed that I was to stay in this room and on no account was I to try to go out. My weapons were removed and, to leave no doubt in my mind as to my status, the door was bolted from the outside when my escort departed.

This was not the way I considered a British officer should be treated and the next time my guard returned I protested strongly, only to get the usual answer that it was being done for my own safety. I had no excuse for going out to relieve myself for, as in many houses in Albania, this need was provided for by a small, wooden, box-like cabin with a hole in the floor, which protruded over the outside wall. The livestock lived below, and nothing was wasted. I considered escaping through this aperture, but even if I had got out without hurting myself in the jump down, I had no idea where I was, where to go, and whether the Albanians I met would be friends or enemies.

During the day my guard came in with food, and sometimes stayed to talk, but for most of the time I was alone. I lay on the floor either sleeping or reading the Bible — the only literature I had with me. I read it from cover to cover and appreciated it more than ever before. I was told that the LNÇ representative would soon be coming to see me, but for the week I stayed in this house my spirits sank very low.

---

[5] In a book such as this, it is impossible to trace the past and present history of Albania or enlarge on the growth and organization of the various political movements. A full and brilliant study on these subjects has been written by Captain Julian Amery (*Sons of the Eagle*, published by Macmillan in 1949) which gives details of the growth of the Albanian resistance movements and the methods whereby the Communists were able eventually to gain control of the country, as well as the parts played by the British missions.

At the end of the week there was a commotion outside my house, caused by the arrival of a new *çeta*. Into my room walked Nexhip Vinçani, with whom I had only had a short talk outside Leskovik. We talked for over two hours, in French, and I discovered that there was still a suspicion that I was a Greek spy, but in the end I convinced him that I was indeed a British officer. He promised to take me with him the next day to meet the LNÇ representative who was in the next village.

My stay at Vithkuq was an important turning point, for it was here that my position changed from that of a virtual prisoner to being accepted by the partisans for what I was, and I established a liaison with them that lasted until McLean and I left the country more than six months later.

Vinçani told me that he was in command of all the *çetas* in the area, though he may have been the commissar; it was not easy to identify the exact position or role of Communist leaders in the party's hierarchy or military organization. He was in his late twenties, good-looking, with a quiet manner, and came from a good family. He had studied law at the university in Italy, which accounted for his ability to speak both Italian and French fluently, and I thought he held a very responsible position for someone of his background. His house had been burnt down by the Italians, for whom he expressed a real hatred, and when I taxed him with being a Communist he assured me he was a nationalist. Whatever his leanings, they were certainly of the far left and almost certainly Communist.

He told me details of the Leskovik operation, and claimed that the Italians had lost 200 (killed), including a lieutenant-colonel and a major, and 150 wounded; 4 light machine guns, 35 rifles and 26 boxes of ammunition had been captured, and 12 lorries and 2 armoured cars destroyed. His own losses were 4 killed and 12 wounded. While I was writing down these figures, I asked him why the partisans had not captured Leskovik, to which he replied, 'Monsieur le Capitaine, the bombing was very heavy, and we were forced to withdraw.' I found all his figures suspect, and having seen the bombing, I realized that very little of it was required to deter the partisans.

I felt that the Italian casualties had been grossly exaggerated, though the list of captured material sounded more credible, for I had seen some of it myself. He added that after the action the Italians had burnt their barracks and most of the town, before evacuating it completely. The partisans were now in possession of it, but the Italians had taken strong reprisals, burning four villages.

Vinçani kept his promise, and we left Vithkuq that evening with an escort of fifteen men. I was happy to leave and after a five-hour night-march we reached the village of Voskopojë. After a good night's sleep Vinçani took me for a stroll in the town, which was extremely old, and noted for its great number of Byzantine churches, over sixty in all, but mostly in ruins. Voskopojë had been ravaged and looted many times in its history, by Turks, Greeks and now Italians.

I was put up in a very ancient house whose owner, a remarkable old woman, was alleged to be 120 years old. She was very bent, with a wizened face that had more wrinkles than I had ever seen on a human face. I thought of Rider Haggard's *She*. Though she wore a black shawl on her head, I could see that she had plenty of grey hair; she had good sight and hearing and could walk with the aid of a stick. I watched her sewing busily for most of the day but could not converse with her, as she only spoke the language of the Vlachs. Her two sons, whose ages were alleged to be eighty-five and eighty-two, were living with her. Tall, upright and very active, they acted as host to me, entertaining me with the traditional raki and *meze* and enjoying a good gossip.

The next day I met the representative of the LNÇ; a small, dark man, with shifty eyes and a rather forced jolly manner, he spoke good English, though with a slight American accent. He introduced himself as Skender Dine; later he admitted that it was not his real name, which I discovered much later to be Koço Tashko.[6] He talked freely about his past, stating that he had been educated at Harvard, had at one time served as secretary to Bishop Fan Noli, had worked as secretary at the Albanian Consulate in New York, and knew Mrs Hasluck.

I got on well enough with him at first, for it was a relief to speak English again instead of French, which I found a strain. I quarrelled with him occasionally when he tried a little subtle Communist propaganda on me, and I never quite trusted him.

I asked if I could get a letter to McLean — Skender had already admitted that the LNÇ had heard from him — and he agreed to send anything I wished by courier. McLean did eventually receive my letters, though the seals were always broken and the contents presumably read. We had fortunately arranged a simple code before we left each other, so I was able to write short sentences which I knew the partisans would not understand. Skender added that McLean had received a supply drop, which was encouraging, for I hoped this would put us in a more favourable light with the LNÇ.

Skender now attached himself to me as my personal shadow, and two days later we moved on to another village where I was told we would meet a member of the Central Committee of the LNÇ. The following morning, he arrived. Doctor Ymer Dishnica was an affable man who spoke excellent French, having been educated at a medical college in Lyons. Dark and

---
[6] Purged in 1960.

cleanshaven, he gave the impression of being capable, clever, and a fanatical Communist. He made no attempt to hide his very strong views from me, as others did, and I considered him a sincere idealist.

Dishnica told me that there were no longer any doubts about my bona fides, and that the LNÇ would help us to receive drops of arms and supplies; he offered to send a *çeta* with me to McLean's headquarters, giving me at the same time a letter from McLean. The seals were broken and stuck up again, Dishnica remarking that it had been opened by mistake. In his letter McLean sounded rather depressed, for up to then he had heard neither from Cairo, the LNÇ, nor me. On the strength of this, I felt that the sooner I rejoined McLean and told him my news, the better. Although neither Dishnica nor myself knew the whereabouts of McLean's HQ, I set off the next day with Skender Dine and a fifteen strong *çeta*, for the first two hours being accompanied by a female *çeta* lustily singing partisan songs with a distinct Russian flavour. Our march of over nine and a half hours followed some of the steepest mountain tracks I had yet encountered, and it became clear that Dine was a townsman rather than a mountaineer.

Our destination turned out to be the village of Leshnjë, perched halfway up the side of a very steep mountain. It was an attractive spot with magnificent views. Walnut and cherry trees were dotted about on the terraces where the maize was growing; mountain streams sparkled as they tumbled down the precipitous and rugged mountains that towered above; I was told that there was a small plateau on top of the mountain and hoped it might make a dropping zone. Below the village, a large valley spread eastwards; this was the way we had come, and the great forests of beech gave a friendly green colouring to the grey and hostile background of the savage mountains.

The house I was allotted belonged to three brothers of the Ylli family. Fine-looking men, all about six foot two inches tall, with fierce-looking moustaches, they wore the traditional Albanian clothes comprising a white fez, a black and white embroidered waistcoat, the baggy Moslem trousers, and socks of vivid colours in which gold and silver thread had been woven. Unfortunately, they were not all that honest, and we were continually missing pieces of our equipment or personal possessions. One of them was the father of Kahreman Ylli, a senior commissar whom we met later.

I waited a week in Leshnjë for McLean, who was reported to be moving in my direction; during this time Gjin Marku arrived, who was the commissar of the Skrapar area. I took an immediate liking to him, for not only was he the first partisan who seemed to be genuinely friendly and ready to help, but he had a real sense of humour, as well as a fine record of bravery in action against the Italians. I asked him to pass a letter to McLean, which actually reached him quickly; later, when I asked him to produce certain information about the Kuçovë oilfields, which I knew was wanted in Cairo, he promised to do so and later produced excellent reports. I told him I wanted to reconnoitre the neighbourhood to select possible dropping grounds and caves for storage. He came with me and for four days we toured the area, while I made notes of likely places. By staying away from the village we gave our hosts a respite from feeding us, for the standard of food had been falling rapidly as the days passed, and we took this as a hint that we were overstaying our welcome, though Gjin Marku complained about the food to the Ylli brothers. He said they were rich and could well afford to feed us better.

On the first day of our tour I was taken to visit Mestan Ujaniku, the leader of the local *çeta*; he was a fine-looking old man who was reputed to have been an outlaw all his life — an honourable profession in Albania. He now wore an imposing array of self-awarded medals and was apt to sign himself 'Commander-in-Chief of the Albanian Army'. He had a great white moustache and greeted me with a kiss on both cheeks — a painful experience since he had a hard stubble of beard. Strangely enough, beards in Albania were customarily worn only by priests and outlaws. Ujaniku was very liberal with his raki, of which he was a keen devotee.

The following day I bought a riding mule for myself costing five sovereigns, and I christened her Fanny (as we always referred to our mentor in Cairo as Fanny Hasluck). Fanny had a very sweet nature and I became devoted to her; she carried me everywhere for the next six months of my stay in Albania. On leaving the country, I handed her over to Alan Hare of the Life Guards. While on leave in England, I sent a signal asking news of Fanny. It was a very severe winter, and our mission at the time was not only on the run from the Germans but was very short of food. Even so, Hare could not have been a true cavalryman, as his reply was short and to the point: 'Have eaten Fanny'.

Skender Dine, Gjin Marku and I stayed in four different villages, and I was able to observe, as well as learn from my escort, a number of Albanian customs. The most important concerned the laws of hospitality. On arrival at a house the guests would be met at the front door by the host, who immediately relieved them of their weapons, which he would usually hang on a wall of the guest room. This gesture meant that from then on, the host took upon himself the responsibility for his guests' lives. I slightly cheated over this custom, for in addition to the big Colt .45 automatic in my belt, I always had a small .25 that fitted into a hip pocket without showing.

Besa was the Albanian expression for these laws. If, to his unending shame, a guest was killed while under his protection, the host would then have a blood feud with the murderer and his family. Until this was avenged, the host could not clear himself of this dishonour, and his neighbours at meals would even show their disapproval or contempt for him by passing the coffee to him under their knees (a symbolic action implying 'I piss in it').

The peasants whose houses we stayed in had a much lower standard of living than those who lived in the bigger towns. Built of grey, locally quarried stone and red roof tiles, very few of them had windows on the ground floor. On entry, two reasons for this became apparent: the ground floor was usually occupied by livestock — sheep, goats, chickens and very occasionally a mule or a cow; and it had defensive advantages, for entry to the house was limited to the door, and with no ground floor windows an enemy was unable to creep up and shoot into the house. Wooden stairs led to the upper floor, which was normally divided into two large rooms — one for the guests, and the other for the family. The entire family slept in the latter, and the women, whom we seldom saw in Moslem houses, did their cooking there. In the richer houses the windows were of glass; others only had wooden shutters, but all had thick iron grills. Wells or streams in the villages provided water; paraffin lamps or candles were the only source of light at night, apart from the fire.

As one entered the house the host led the way upstairs to the guest room, usually the larger of the two. Normally it was sparsely furnished except for some rugs on the floor and a large wooden chest containing blankets. Coffee was served immediately, and in cold weather glowing embers were brought in from the fire in the other room, and a blazing fire would soon be burning. While drinking coffee, the guests had to indicate whether they wanted to stay the night by removing their boots, whereupon the host would shout to the womenfolk to prepare a meal. If it was an Orthodox or a Catholic house, a girl or woman would come in at this stage to wash, and sometimes massage, the feet of the more honoured guests — I found this a great relief after a long march. In a Moslem house this duty was usually performed by the son of the house, or some rugged old warrior servant.

Before the meal could be served bread had to be baked, and a sheep or a chicken killed and cooked. This naturally took a long time, and it was not unusual to sit for anything up to four hours waiting for the meal to arrive. During this wait raki and *meze* were kept in constant circulation, the *meza* consisting of lumps of cheese, raw onions, cloves of garlic, cucumber in yoghurt, hard boiled eggs, and the liver and other intestines of the animal that had just been killed. The host clearly enjoyed this interval, gossiping and exchanging news, and his natural curiosity was particularly aroused by the presence of a foreigner in his house. Many times I arrived at a house dead tired after a long day's march, and it was as much as I could do to stay awake; but to go to sleep would have been considered bad manners and I had to force myself to sit up and appear to take a polite interest in the conversation, even though I did not understand it. It was only the raki that kept me going. A very strong spirit distilled from plums or grapes, it had a remarkable effect in overcoming tiredness.

When the meal was ready, a large round table, about five feet in diameter and about nine inches high, would be brought in and placed in the centre of the room. The host would then seat the senior guest in the place of honour, whereupon everyone would move over to the table, each man facing the back of his neighbour and turning his back on the other; in this way, as many as fifteen people could sit at one table.

The food would already be on the table, usually loaves of bread made from maize (*buke*), dishes of yoghurt (*kos*) usually made from sheep's milk, and beans (*fasule*) of a similar type to Heinz baked beans; the main dish was meat boiled in its own juice, sometimes with a few grains of rice.

We ate most dishes with the fingers of our right hands, but a spoon was provided for the more liquid ones, and this was the only piece of cutlery. There were no individual plates and we conveyed the food direct from the communal dish to our mouths. There was an art in eating quickly without spilling too much, for the dishes emptied fast and the slower feeder often went short. McLean used to say that I was good at table tactics. Once the dishes were empty the meal was over, the guests returned to their original positions, and a member of the family removed the table and swept the crumbs and any leftovers through a hole in the centre of the floor to fall among the animals who dwelt below. Once this was done, conversation flagged, mattresses were brought in, the blankets laid out, and in a short time the only noise would be the crackling of the fire and loud snores.

On leaving the house the following morning, the host would usually accompany his guests for the first mile or so of their journey, and it was not until he had said his farewell and turned for home that the *beza* was no longer binding.[7]

---

[7] Albanian customs are many and complicated. A comprehensive book on this subject is *The Unwritten Law of Albania*, by Margaret Hasluck, published by the Cambridge University Press in 1954.

On the fourth day of our tour, we received news that McLean and his party were approaching Leshnjë, so next morning we hurried back and found them already there. We were all happy and relieved to see each other again, McLean having had a very frustrating time at Drymades, for his communications with Cairo had been bad; Bedri Spahiu had been particularly obstructive right up to the last minute — when presumably he had received orders from the LNÇ to co-operate — and McLean had received no letters from me until a few days before his arrival at Leshnjë.

Chapter V: Supply drops and our first success

While at Leshnjë a signal came from Cairo to say that we would shortly receive our first supply drops, so we moved higher up the mountain to be nearer the dropping zone. Mt Leshnjë was one of the prominent features of the Zaloshnjë mountains, a range running north and south whose highest peak, Mount Tomorr, could be seen to our north; it was a sacred mountain of ancient times and one of the highest in Albania, rising to about 7500 feet.

The DZ that I had selected was on a small plateau some two hours climb above the village; our HQ was in a wooden shepherd's hut, with only one room, mud floors and plenty of fleas. Though less comfortable than in the village, we were pleased to be away from the prying villagers who were becoming a nuisance, giving us no privacy and stealing our food and kit.

A supply drop reception committee needed a number of men on the spot to light the signal fires and keep them burning, and mules onto which the stores could be loaded after the men had collected them, so they could be carried away quickly. The main difficulty was to get them to the DZ at the right time without any loss of security; for although we were warned of impending sorties by Cairo some days ahead, changes caused by the weather, poor communications, or other commitments often caused last-minute postponements or cancellations.

It became my job in the mission to organize the reception of all our supply drops, and of the more than thirty drops during our first period in Albania, well over half were postponed and others cancelled. This entailed waiting all through the bitterly cold night, straining our ears for the aircraft that never came, for we never lit the fires until we were sure it was one of ours; in the early hours of the morning, when it was too late for any aircraft to come, we returned cold and disconsolate, swearing at Cairo because we had not been informed. It was not, of course, Cairo's fault, for communications between the RAF in Derna and our rear link in Cairo, and between Cairo and ourselves, did not allow time for word to reach us soon enough if a sortie was cancelled. Even worse was an aeroplane appearing overhead without previous warning and finding us unprepared. This is precisely what happened on our first drop.

On 23 June we were all ready for our first drop; mules had been bought or hired, the local commissar, Ramiz Aranitas, had promised to produce men, given a day's notice. He had incidentally provided me with two men as a bodyguard — Reta, who stayed with me for several months, and Ali, who did not, for reasons that will appear later.

For the first three nights, we all waited forlornly. It was obvious that no aircraft would come, for the mountain top was enveloped in thick cloud, though we could not signal Cairo this in time to cancel the aircraft; on the third night we heard the Halifax above the clouds searching in vain for the fires. The fourth night our hopes rose, for conditions were perfect; to our disappointment and annoyance the aircraft did not come, and the next day a signal told us that the weather in Derna was so bad that all sorties had to be cancelled. The signal told us to stand down our reception committee; we would be informed later of the date of the next attempt to drop.

McLean left next day to meet some of the LNÇ Central Council at a nearby village; before leaving he asked me to pay out some money to Ramiz Aranitas for his *çeta*, the reception committee, and the hire of mules and mulemen. Ramiz stayed to supper with me, and before he left I gave him 200 sovereigns. Soon after, I heard a shot but thought nothing of it; Albanians were always letting off their rifles when celebrating feast days or weddings, or when drunk, or just in error. I crawled into my sleeping bag on the floor.

I was woken at two in the morning by the sound of an aircraft overhead; I recognized the engine as that of a Halifax which was obviously looking for our DZ, although we had received no signal to expect a sortie. Shouting to Williamson, Reta, and Ali, I rushed out in my pyjamas and bare feet to light the signal fires, but of course they were damp. It took Williamson, Reta, and myself — of Ali there was no sign — over half an hour to light the eleven fires which were laid out in the form of the letter V. Meanwhile, two aircraft — by now a second one had arrived — circled overhead. Finally the fires were all lit, the recognition signals had been flashed by torch, and the two Halifaxes made their runs, dropping their containers accurately enough, although the free drops[8] gave us a fright as they thudded to the ground much too near for comfort, the Dannert wire making exactly the same whistling noise as a bomb. After the last run, they flashed their lights and headed home for Africa.

I returned to the hut and got dressed, my bare feet and legs having been badly stung by nettles, and sent Reta off to summon Ramiz Aranitas to bring up the reception party and mules as soon as possible to collect the supplies; an Italian

---

[8] Free drops were bundles dropped from the aircraft without parachutes such as battledress, blankets, boots etc. In the deep snow of the winter they even dropped jerricans of petrol, though most of these broke on hitting the ground.

airfield only eight miles away made it essential that the DZ be cleared of all parachutes and containers before first light in case a reconnaissance aircraft spotted them.

Ten minutes later, Reta returned in a high state of excitement to say that he had found the body of Ramiz lying on the track about half a mile away; he had been shot dead. It was not until the next day that the mystery was solved; it turned out that my bodyguard Ali had seen me hand over the 200 sovereigns to Ramiz, lain in ambush for him, killed him — that was the shot I had heard — and made off with the 200 sovereigns; we never saw him again. I was relieved that Ali did not share the secret, known only to McLean and Williamson, that I kept 400 sovereigns buried in the floor under my sleeping bag.

Sovereigns played a vital part in our existence, for without them we could have done nothing. During our first stay in Albania our mission received by parachute, and accounted for, over 30,000 sovereigns. Some of the bags in which they came bore the Bank of England seal and certificates stating that they had been checked over forty years ago — the dates were stamped on them — and most of the coins bore the head of Queen Victoria; we sometimes also received French or Italian gold napoleons.

During one of the supply drops at Leshnjë a parachute failed to open, as sometimes happened, and the container burst on hitting the ground. We knew it should have contained a bag of 1000 sovereigns, so made a very thorough search of the ground next morning and recovered over 900 of them. The majority were very bent and buckled, and the locals refused to accept them in spite of our efforts to persuade them that they still contained the same amount of gold as normal ones. We managed to keep them some months until we could send them back to our base in Bari by sea, after we had established a secret landing beach later.

The following day we received the belated signal to say that the two aircraft were coming after all, and furthermore that two more were coming that very night. It took the whole day to unpack the containers and store all the supplies away, but by now the reception party had joined us and we were all prepared for the next drop. This took place without incident, and the dropping was very accurate, but we discovered that all the boots that I had especially requested for the partisans turned out to be size six, and only suitable for children. Shades of the Crimean War!

We were joined that day by Corporal Bell, a new wireless operator who arrived complete with his W/T set, having taken three weeks to walk to us from Greece, though I could not understand why he had not been dropped to us direct. He was a very welcome reinforcement to the mission; McLean had asked for another W/T station as one between us was inadequate as we separated so often. From now on, one set could always be at the mission's base, and the other could be taken wherever it was needed. Although we were not allowed, for security reasons, to communicate directly with each other, we could always pass messages through Cairo.

Immediately after the supply drops, and this became routine later on, the partisans and other hangers-on descended on us like flies, hanging round the HQ, snooping, poking into stores, begging for arms and equipment, pilfering or scrounging what they could, and being a thorough nuisance. On this occasion Mestan Ujaniku was the first to arrive, followed shortly by the commissars for the Valona (Vlore) and Berat areas. They all wanted arms, usually the same ones to be more difficult, but I refused to issue any until I had listed them and divided them into three groups for the Valona, Berat and Korçë *çetas*. When this was done, I handed them all over to Kahreman Ylli and made him sign for them; this stood me in good stead later on.

By now McLean had returned from his meeting, where it had been agreed that we would move to a new base nearer Korçë; there the LNÇ would produce *çetas* for us to train and equip; these would form the nucleus of the First Partisan Brigade.

Before moving we had to collect a large number of mules, some of which we hired and others we bought for sums ranging from four to six sovereigns. Those we hired came with their owners who were usually Vlachs, a nomad tribe said to be of Rumanian origin, reputedly descended from the Ancient Dacians and found throughout the Balkans. Speaking a Latin language of their own, they kept to themselves, living in encampments rather than villages, in the summer months moving with their mules to the good grazing in the mountains, and down to the valleys and plains again in the winter. Mules and saddlery were their livelihood; they treated their mules well, taking trouble in the loading and fitting of saddles, unlike most Albanian peasants. Providing we paid them well they remained loyal, but their reliability deteriorated the nearer they came to any active operations, for fighting had no part in their character; to be fair, when they joined us they did not expect to find themselves being bombed or pursued by hostile Italians or Germans.

For our move from Leshnjë we had sixty mules, and it was a day's march to our new base at the village of Shtyllë. Apart from one mule falling over a precipice and being killed, it was a pleasant march through country ranging from barren and rocky mountains to thick beech forests with running streams; at one time we passed a maze of trenches, a reminder of the fighting between the French and the Austrians in the 1914-18 war.

Shtyllë was a village of some fifty houses situated at the head of two valleys, one of which descended towards Vithkuq and the Korçë plain, while the other led to a wide area that eventually became our DZ, which could only be reached by a mule track. A motorable road led towards Vithkuq. For our new HQ, the LNÇ had allotted us a school which had been converted from a disused mosque. It was ideal in every way, for we were isolated from the village and had a good view down both valleys and a good stream for water ran nearby. It contained three rooms, which we divided into living quarters, a storeroom, and the wireless room; as such it was adequate, though on the small side.

Two days after our arrival, Nexhip Vinçani appeared with the news that he was going to attack Përmet and asked if he could borrow one of our 20 mm guns, which could be used in an antiaircraft or ground role. As I was the only person trained to fire it, I had a good excuse to go with him, for we wanted an eyewitness to partisan actions to confirm or refute their claims. As gun-bearers for the Breda he lent me two Italian Army deserters, still in their army uniform; they were big tough men and turned out to be conscripted Yugoslavs.

We made a forced march of fourteen hours before reaching a hill overlooking Përmet, and for the first two days of the attack I was in a position from which I could shoot at every Italian aircraft that came within range. I never hit one, though the number of near misses may well have discouraged the Italian pilots from further low level action, for the 20 mm shells from the Breda fired tracer bullets, which burst with small puffs of smoke that were easy to see. I could sense that the attack was not going well, and the partisans seemed to be confining themselves to long-range fire on the Italian barracks. Good news came in at one stage that an Italian column had been successfully ambushed in the Gorge of Këlcyrë.

On the third evening, Vinçani told me that they were planning a night attack on an Italian camp at a place called Kuqar, near Përmet, and I offered to come too. I attended an operations conference that evening at which all the commissars spoke at length, but from what I gathered at the end of it they had evolved little in the way of a plan. After dark we set off for Kuqar with Vinçani leading, myself next, the two Yugoslavs carrying the Breda, and Pellump Dishnica, the commissar, bringing up the rear. I had blissfully assumed that our own troops were in advance of us, but suddenly a hail of small arms fire opened up on us from our front and mortar bombs started landing around us, so we dived for cover, whereupon small arms fire opened up on us from the rear. For two hours we were pinned down in this uncomfortable position between the Italians and partisans, who were firing wildly at each other, though most of their shots went high. This seemed a somewhat embarrassing position for the commander of the operation to find himself in, and I told Vinçani so. He agreed and decided to withdraw, for which I was much relieved, and we returned through our own men who by now had stopped shooting at us. The partisans had two men killed, one wounded, and one missing; it seemed to me that the whole operation had been badly mismanaged, for there had been no previous reconnaissance of the Italian positions which proved to be much further forward than the partisans had anticipated. They claimed to have inflicted heavy casualties on the Italians, but I certainly did not see any, and doubted it.

After two more days of long-range sniping at Përmet, the operation was abandoned. The final result was similar to the Leskovik action — the partisans had failed to capture the town, but they had been successful in ambushing the relieving columns, though their claims of enemy casualties were wildly extravagant. As in the case of Leskovik the Italians burnt their barracks, set fire to the houses in the town, and withdrew their garrison to a more secure base.

On my way back I saw smoke from other burning villages, and I assumed they had been set on fire by the Italians as reprisals; I was wrong, for I came across Safet Butka and his Balli Kombëtar *çeta*, who told me that it was the village of Barmash I had seen burning, and that it had been started by the Germans. He said they had burnt women and children alive in their homes and shot them when they tried to escape; he added that a German division had just arrived at Korçë from Florina. This was our first news of Germans in Albania.

Professor Safet Butka, who came from a patriotic Albanian family, had been a teacher of Albanian, and later a Director of the Tirana Gymnasium. After the Italian occupation he had been interned in Italy, where he had remained for two years until he had been released in 1942. He then took an active part in the Balli Kombëtar movement and became the commandant of the Ballist *çetas* in the Korçë area. He appeared very depressed when I met him, and he complained bitterly that the British were arming the partisans, and not their real allies, the Balli Kombëtar; to this I replied that as soon as they had proved that they were willing to fight the Germans and Italians, we would give them arms. Sometime after, I heard that he had been besieged in a house by the partisans, and that rather than fall into their hands he had committed suicide. Thus, the Balli Kombëtar lost a good leader, and Albania one of the first patriots to become a victim of the Communists.

We remained at Shtyllë for the next two months, and received a large number of supply drops, including a number of British officers and NCOs; meanwhile, we were training the partisans to use the weapons that had been dropped to us. As we handed the weapons over to them, we hoped they would use them in action against the common enemy. We ourselves carried out a number of operations on the Korçë-Leskovik road as it was an important line of communication, continuing as it did to Yannena in Greece.

Flight-Lieutenant Andy Hands RAF, his operator and two paramilitary specialists, Sergeants Jones and Jenkins, were the first party to be dropped. Hands left after a few days to set up a mission in the Dibër area, where he later distinguished himself in carrying out the destruction of some important chrome mines, but Jones and Jenkins stayed with us. Jones was a big red-haired sergeant from the Welsh Guards, and Jenkins a dark, thickset, rugged sergeant from the RASC, who had been a professional footballer; both came from the same street in Liverpool. Close friends, they had joined the Commandos together, came out to the Middle East with Layforce and, on its disbandment, joined SOE. They were a tremendous asset to the mission, for not only were they experts at their jobs, but they could turn their hands to anything. Brave as lions, they had the typical British soldier's sense of humour and a good-natured but total contempt for all foreigners, including the Albanians; whenever there was trouble and our Albanian guards and followers made themselves scarce — as happened on a number of occasions — Jones and Jenkins would always dependably and imperturbably be on hand cracking jokes or making digs at our own superior authorities or our so-called allies.

As we grew in numbers and accommodation grew more cramped, we decided to build a wooden house close to our own. It cost sixty sovereigns to build and we named it 'the barracks'; it had four large rooms and a kitchen, and the whole building was covered by a green camouflaged parachute to make it less conspicuous from the air.

The next drop, on 17 July, brought another BLO, Squadron Leader Tony Neel, RAF, a tall and charming officer whom McLean sent off to the north of the country to join Abas Kupi, the leader of the Zogist *çetas*. The following night I was in charge of the reception party at another supply drop, not without incident.

Two aircraft were expected, and as soon as I heard the Halifax in the distance I had the signal fires lit; by now I was attuned to hearing aircraft at a distance and recognizing their engines. The first Halifax arrived, made its drops successfully, and flew off to base. The second Halifax had arrived and was making its first run over the DZ when I distinctly heard the noise of a third aircraft, which sounded very much like one of the Italian Savoia or Caproni three-engined bombers. I immediately shouted in French to everybody on the ground to run for cover, which I did myself; unfortunately I forgot that Duffy, who had been in the centre of the DZ flashing the recognition signals with his torch, could not speak French. The third aircraft now flew straight over the DZ and dropped a stick of bombs that blew out some of the fires, luckily missing Duffy, who wasted no time in removing himself. For the next five minutes we watched fascinated as the Halifax made three more runs dropping stores, followed immediately by the Italian bomber dropping bombs, both apparently oblivious to the other. Eventually they all flew off, and we immediately started to clear the ground. Nobody had been hurt, though some of the containers had been damaged by the bombs and were hard to open. It was essential that the ground be cleared by first light, for an Italian reconnaissance aircraft would certainly be over the next morning and could not help seeing the bomb craters, which from their size we estimated to come from 500 lb bombs. While this was going on, the locals took the opportunity of looting some of our supplies including the specially marked container containing our mail, newspapers (I usually received *The Tatler, Picture Post, Horse and Hound* and occasional copies of *The Times*), food luxuries, and often including a bottle of whisky. I was already in a foul temper when a peasant approached me and said he was the owner of the land where the bombs had dropped and wanted compensation; I told him to apply to the Italians!

No reconnaissance plane did appear the next morning, to our surprise and relief, and we learned later that the bomber had crashed on landing at Korçë airfield the same night and all the crew had been killed; presumably they never had time to pass on any information about our DZ.

Some days later McLean returned, and we received the first of many visits from the *Shtab* — the General Staff of the LNÇ, of whom the two leading members were Mehmet Shehu and Enver Hoxha. Mehmet Shehu was a short, wiry, dark, sallow-faced man of about thirty who seldom smiled except at other people's misfortunes. He spoke good English, was very capable, and had far more military knowledge than most other Albanians. After early education at the American school in Tirana he had attended a military college in Naples, from which he was expelled for Communist activities; a course at the Officers' School in Tirana was followed by Spain in 1938, where he joined the 'Garibaldi' International Brigade, and became Acting Commander of the Fourth Battalion. When the brigade withdrew into France in 1939, he was interned for three years. On his release he returned to Albania where he joined the partisan movement, shortly becoming a member of the Communist Party Committee in the Valona area. By the time we met him, he was the commissar of all the partisan forces in the area.

He had a reputation for bravery, ruthlessness, and cruelty — he boasted that he had personally cut the throats of seventy Italian *carabinieri* who had been taken prisoner. I got on with him at first, for as soldiers we had something in common; but he did little to conceal his dislike of all things British, and my relations with him deteriorated. At one of our meetings with the *Shtab*, he made wild accusations against us, swearing that we had given all the arms dropped to us in Albania to the Balli Kombëtar, leaving none for the partisans. In reply I drew out of my briefcase a sheaf of lists of weapons I had handed over to the partisans, with the signed receipts attached; I took my time reading these out aloud in front of the *Shtab*, to Shehu's discomfort and fury, and he never forgave me. Later on, when the First Partisan Brigade put up as despicable an exhibition of cowardice as I had yet seen, I had my last words with Shehu, and they were far from polite. After the war, he became Prime Minister of Albania and held that position until he was reported to have committed suicide in 1981.

Enver Hoxha was an entirely different character — a big man with too much flesh and a flabby handshake. He was not a military man although he had military pretensions, but he was more sociable than Shehu, and spoke with us in fluent French. He may have disliked us, but at least he concealed his feelings, whereas with Shehu you could feel the hostility.

Hoxha was about thirty-five years old. He had been educated in Gjirokastër Grammar School, the *lycée* in Korçë, and the

University of Montpellier in France, which he was compelled to leave for failing his exams. He went on to Brussels and Paris to study law, though he never graduated, and returned to Albania to become a French teacher at the State Gymnasium in Tirana; he was later transferred to the *lycée* in Korçë, still as a teacher of French. We always knew him as 'Professor' Enver Hoxha — presumably he derived this title from his teaching appointments. He gave up teaching in 1940 to run a tobacconist's shop in Tirana, which became a Communist cell and rendezvous for anti-government elements; after the founding of the Albanian Communist Party in 1941, he became the Secretary-General to the Party Central Committee, which was probably the position he still held when we first met him.

I got on well with Hoxha, even though he was inclined to bluster and lose his temper at our endless meetings. I took delight in teasing him about his politics, and the more Communist propaganda he aimed at me, the more right-wing, capitalist and imperialist I became. Once, we were standing in front of a war map of the world while he lectured me on how he would like to see the world after the war — Communist, of course, all over. Turning to me, he said, 'How would you like to see the world, Monsieur le Capitaine?'; to which I replied, 'I too would like to see this map painted red all over, but not the sort of red you mean.'[9] He seemed puzzled, but I let him think it out on his own. Hoxha had quite a sense of humour, and over a glass of raki could be cheerful and amusing, in contrast to his dour and morose companion Mehmet Shehu. He became President of Albania after the war — a position he held until his death in 1985.

---

[9] Before the Second World War, the British Empire was coloured red in maps of the world.

While we were at Shtyllë relations with Skender Dine grew strained, for our NCOs reported to us that he was trying to indoctrinate them with communist propaganda; after a bloody row with McLean he left, never to return. In his place the LNÇ appointed a young man called Fred Nosi as their Liaison Officer. He was the nephew of Lef Nosi, Mrs Hasluck's friend, and he had been educated at the American College in Tirana run by Harry T. Fultz, probably the best-known and best-loved American ever to have been in Albania. Nosi spoke good English, and we used him as interpreter on most occasions; though pleasant enough, we knew him to be a convinced Communist and the official LNÇ spy in our midst, reporting on our activities and contacts.

Nexhip Vinçani had given me a list of his *çetas*, the names of their leaders, their strength and their weapons. From these *çetas* a number were chosen to come to us for training, after which we would issue them with more weapons. Eventually these *çetas* were amalgamated to form the First Partisan Brigade. The first *çeta* to arrive was that of Petrit Dume, with whom I got on well, for he was young, enthusiastic, and keen to learn. While Duffy, Jones and Jenkins trained them in mines and demolitions, McLean and I trained them in such heavier weapons as the 81 mm mortars, and the 20 and 47 mm guns.

Çetas of the Korçë area, June 1943

Commandant: NEXHIP VINÇANI
Commissar: PELLUMB DISHNICA

Leskovik:
SULO KOZELLI, 25 men, 1 HMG, 2 LMG

Ersekë:
PETRIT DUME, 40 men, 4 LMG, 2 mortars

Bilisht:
DEMIR, 25 men 2 LMG
SHEEQET, 25 men 2 LMG
MITO, 32 men 2 LMG
BATO, 35 men 1 LMG
TEFIK CAKONJE, 40 men 2 LMG

Pogradec:
LIKO, 35 men 2 LMG
MURAT, 27 men, 1 LMG
RESHID, 60 men, 3 LMG, 1 mortar

Gore:
TEKI KOLANECI, 44 men, 3 LMG, 2 mortars
ALI VINÇANI, 45 men, 2 LMG, 1 mortar
ASLLAN GURA, 30 men, 1 LMG
AGUSH, 30 men, 1 LMG

Opar:
SHABAN, 35 men, 3 LMG
LUSHNI SELSA, 25 men, 2 LMG

Total of active bands
Men 570, Heavy machine guns (HMG) 1, Light machine guns (LMG) 33, Mortars 6.

These were the active bands and did not include the territorial or village bands who remained stationary, or the reserves. Both these had rifles and could be called upon when necessary. Not all these *çetas* took part in the Leskovik action, as about 25 per cent had to be left in their areas for security reasons against Italian reaction or for political reasons in case of reaction by the Balli Kombëtar.

This shows the strength and armament of the Korçë area *çetas* before they had received any arms or financial assistance from the British Military Mission.

About this time, I heard that the Italians were in Voskopojë, so I walked the few miles over to see what was happening, accompanied by an Italian Air Force deserter who was attached to our HQ. On arrival we found the whole town in flames, the Italians having withdrawn after setting it on fire for what was alleged to be the fifteenth time in its history. The Italians had met no opposition, and the partisans who were there had withdrawn without firing a shot. When I met Vinçani in the town, I asked him why the partisans had not fought; he replied that his battalion was 'doing a flanking movement to cut them off', which I did not believe. It was obvious that they had run away, and I became somewhat offensive, telling him that his battalion was not a battalion but a guerrilla band, and a damned bad one at that, and that the sooner he stopped trying to be a general instead of a guerrilla leader the better; he looked very dejected and we parted on bad terms.

The following day I went down the valley and blew up a bridge on the road between Shtyllë and Vithkuq, to ensure that we could not be surprised by the Italians if they suddenly decided to come down the road in armoured cars or trucks. I then walked down the road through the foothills to lay mines on the main road that ran in the valley below which connected Korçë and Leskovik and was in daily use by the Italians and Germans. The operation was a failure. In the first place Reta, my bodyguard, ran away, leaving my other bodyguard, Shterian, and myself to work alone. Then the road was so hard that our small hand pick was not up to digging a hole deep enough in which to lay the mines: as I left, I was conscious that they were badly laid and easy to spot; we could only hope for the best. We waited some hours before the first lorry, a German one, appeared but someone in the lorry spotted the disturbance on the road and it stopped. A few minutes later, a convoy arrived from which four German officers appeared and one of them lifted the mines and then all four walked gingerly along the road on tiptoe for about half a mile looking for mines. I enjoyed this and made a mental note to booby trap the next ones I laid, for I knew there were none; although we had done no damage to the convoy we had delayed it for some hours, and I hoped the mines had upset the drivers' nerves.

On my return, I found that Duffy had been more successful; his mines had blown up a German lorry, unfortunately filled with Albanians.

Two nights later we had an alarming incident; McLean, Williamson, and I all slept in the same long and narrow room as the W/T set; since we slept on the floor, we had to step over each other if we wanted to move around. In the middle of the night, I heard shouts and awoke to see two people fighting in the centre of the room; pulling my pistol from under my pillow I aimed it at them, wondering which one to shoot, until I recognized that they were McLean and Williamson. McLean was winning, for Williamson was yelling as McLean had him by the throat, meanwhile making queer animal-like grunts and groans himself; suddenly McLean must have realized whom he was throttling and stopped. It turned out that Williamson had got up to go outside to relieve himself and had stepped on McLean by mistake. McLean was at that moment having a nightmare in which he thought that the Italian Air Force deserter was a double agent and had been sent to murder us. When Williamson had tripped over him McLean had leapt to his feet, and, thinking that Williamson was the Italian, had nearly strangled him.

Under these conditions we were, to a certain extent, living on our nerves, and, as a result of the heavy mental strain, nightmares were not uncommon. I suffered from them myself and continued to do so for some time after the war had ended. Strangely enough the Italian deserter disappeared the next day, and we were worried that he had returned to the Italians to give us away; but we had misjudged the poor fellow, for we found out that he had been murdered by a partisan who wanted his boots.

On 10 August, I left Shtyllë to earn out an ambush with a Ballist *çeta*. This had been arranged by McLean with Safet Butka to test, among other things, the willingness of the Balli Kombëtar to fight the Italians and Germans. Fred Nosi and our attached partisans were strongly opposed to this move and took steps to thwart it. The date fixed for the ambush was 12 August; McLean and I were keen grouse shots and agreed that this would be an appropriate day to open the season.

Leaving Shtyllë with two guides and the faithful Yugoslavs carrying the Breda, I arrived after some hours' march at the village of Kurtes, where I found the whole *çeta*, some 200 men strong, drawn up for my inspection under Captain Qemal Burimi. He and I both made speeches, then spent the rest of the day in making our plan. Unlike the partisans, who always thought they knew best, Captain Burimi was prepared to listen to my advice and even take it. Next morning, we moved nearer the road, not far from the burnt-out village of Barmash, where we made a close reconnaissance in daylight. On our way back to the village, we had reached the top of some steep cliffs when we met a *çeta* of about thirty partisans sitting on top who had clearly been watching us. I recognized the leader, Petrit Dume. 'What are you doing here?' I asked. 'We are going to ambush the road tonight,' he replied. 'Where?' I asked. 'Down there' — he pointed to the corner of the road where Burimi and I had decided to lay the ambush; he had obviously seen us there.

It seemed clear to me that he had been put up to this by the LNÇ, probably on information from Fred Nosi; the object, without doubt, was to prevent the Balli Kombëtar from carrying out an ambush that would give them credit in the eyes of the British and give the lie to the LNÇ allegations that they were collaborating with the Germans and Italians.

I grew angry at the thought that our plans might come to nought and said to Dume, 'You cannot lay an ambush here tonight as I am doing one with Captain Burimi and his *çeta*.' Dume replied that he had been given his orders and intended to carry them out. 'If you do an ambush here tonight,' I told him, 'I promise you that the LNÇ will receive no more arms or money from the British Mission, and we will give all we get to the Balli Kombëtar.' I had no authority to make this threat, but it was all I could think up on the spur of the moment. However, it seemed to work for, muttering oaths (probably directed at me), Dume led his *çeta* off down a track in the direction of Korçë. I wondered what his next move would be; I felt sure he had orders to wreck our plans and would attempt to do so. In the event he did nothing, and we saw no more of him.

We had found an ideal spot for the ambush, where the road had been cut out of the side of a very steep mountain and had numerous bends; the mountain itself dropped sheer below the road into a river, and a steep cliff above the road prevented anyone on it from escaping or taking cover. The hills rose again the other side of the river, and I planned to deploy the *çeta* on these hills; they would be about two hundred yards from the road, with a gully between them and the enemy.

During the night I took a party of ten men with sixteen mines down onto the road, intending to lay the mines in two groups of eight about 250 yards apart but out of sight of each other on either side of a bend in the road. When we had laid the first four mines a Halifax flew over, one of the Albanians shouted, 'a lorry! a lorry!', and the entire party ran away, never to reappear. I therefore had to dig the holes and lay the remaining mines myself, which took over four hours, luckily without any disturbance, and finished just before daybreak at about five in the morning. I climbed the hill to the *çeta* positions, exhausted and in a foul temper; there I found a very apologetic Captain Burimi. 'My men have not had much training,' he explained. I agreed.

We took up our positions, and a short while later my temper was cooled by the fine sight of a big German half-tracked troop carrier approaching from the direction of Korçë; better still, on nearing I saw it was towing an 88 mm gun. Some of the *çeta*, now back in their positions near me, shouted 'a tank! a tank!' and ran away, but the less timid of their companions stayed with me; otherwise, we were all ready and in position, and I had both my camera and the Breda gun trained on the spot where I had laid the mines. As the carrier drew closer, every one of us held his breath; then it went up on the mines with a flash of orange flame followed by a cloud of smoke, and the sound of the explosion echoed through the hills. I had taken a photograph as the mines exploded; by the force of the explosion, I estimated that all eight mines must have detonated at once. Once the smoke had cleared, everyone opened fire on the troop carrier; I exchanged my camera for the 20 mm Breda and was delighted to see several of my shots score direct hits. A few Germans jumped out of the carrier and tried to run back down the road, but all were shot, and the others tried to take cover behind the carrier. In time the shooting stopped, and a silence followed, only broken by the groans of some of the wounded. I asked Captain Burimi to send some of his men down to the road to get identifications and to try to push the gun off the road into the riverbed below. A few men then cautiously approached the road, some shots rang out — presumably the wounded being finished off — and the gun was then unhitched and pushed over the side, but the half-track proved impossible to move because most of its front was blown away. After about half an hour, the men returned from the road very pleased with themselves; I was happy too because they had collected the identifications I had wanted and various pieces of loot, and they told me eighteen Germans had been killed. Twelve were dead in the troop carrier, probably killed by the exploding mines; the six lying on the road behind the carrier had been shot. While they were excitedly telling their story, I heard engines and then saw in the distance a large convoy of lorries coming from the direction of Leskovik; this was excellent, for they would blow up on the second group of mines before they could see the wrecked troop carrier. As they approached, I counted twenty-three lorries but on checking that all the *çeta* had moved into their positions was saddened to see that all but about six men, and the two Yugoslavs who appeared to be enjoying themselves immensely, had vanished.

The first lorry went over the mines with a terrific explosion, the whole of the front and the cab disintegrating; I took another photograph. The rest of the convoy immediately halted; two Germans jumped out of the cab of each lorry and ran back down the road while the *çeta* shot at them. Through my binoculars I could see the bodies of five Germans lying by the first lorry, so I proceeded to shoot at the second with my Breda. I hit it with my third shot and it burst into flames, and I did the same to the third lorry. Had the full *çeta* remained in position with me I was convinced the entire convoy could have been destroyed, but after about ten minutes the Germans had reorganized themselves to shoot back, to which we replied; when I spotted a small party starting to climb our hill away on a flank, I considered it time to go, so with my attendant caddies, as I called them, we picked up the Breda and walked away.

Although my opinion of Albanian fighting quality was somewhat low I was very satisfied with the results, for we had killed twenty-three Germans without a casualty to ourselves, taken identifications of the First Alpine Division, destroyed a large troop carrier, one 88 mm gun, and three lorries. With better disciplined and properly trained troops, we certainly could have destroyed the lot.

On my return to Shtyllë, I found that more aeroplanes had been over in addition to the one I had heard when on the road, and a new group of officers had arrived — Major Bill Tilman, Major Gerry Field, Major George Seymour, and Major Peter Kemp.

Of these Bill Tilman was the oldest, and probably the toughest, for he was a mountaineer of considerable repute who had taken part in expeditions in many parts of the world; he was the conqueror of Mount Kamut and had been a member of the 1933, 1936 and 1938 Everest expeditions. About my size, usually described as stocky, with a sharp face and bristly moustache, he was a gunner by profession. He expressed great pleasure at being in Albania because there were so many mountains to climb. Once his mission had been established, he climbed the local mountains every morning before breakfast, to the great discomfiture of his partisan guards who had been given strict orders to accompany him everywhere and not let him out of their sight.[10]

Gerry Field had dropped out of the same aircraft as Tilman, actually managing to be sick as he was coming down in his parachute, which sounded very messy as he came down faster than his vomit.

George Seymour was a tall, thin, military-looking man with a large, fierce looking moustache that curled up at the ends. Originally an officer in the Royal Scots Fusiliers, he had been wounded at the battle of Alamein. He was a regular army officer, as were Tilman and Field, and this was apparent from their appearance, behaviour and conversation.

The fourth member of the party, Peter Kemp, had hit his head on a rock on landing and been slightly concussed. Unlike his three companions he was not a regular officer, nor was he likely to be taken for one, being both unconventional and eccentric. In spite of this, he had probably been involved in more active fighting than his three companions put together. After coming down from Cambridge he had joined the Nationalists in the Spanish Civil War, where he had been severely wounded and decorated for bravery. Obtaining a commission in the British Army at the outbreak of the war as an officer on the General List — owing to his cap badge, we sometimes unkindly referred to his unit as Crosse and Blackwells' Light Infantry — he was recruited by SOE in the early stages of its formation; an officer of his experience was

---

[10] Sadly, it was reported in 1979 that he and his crew vanished without trace on a yacht in the South Atlantic in 1979.

invaluable. He had already seen action in a number of operations, mainly in raids on the French coast, as well as having been involved in several hazardous operations in submarines. He was tall, fair, talkative, very entertaining, rather worried over his health, and he shared with me a liking for good food and drink.

Chapter VI: Formation of 1st Partisan Brigade, retreat, Italian surrender

Our four new officers arrived just in time for the inauguration of the First Partisan Brigade, which took place on a large plain near Vithkuq. About eight hundred partisans were formed up in long lines, complete with all the weapons and equipment that we had given them. Of all ages and shapes they seemed in good heart, enthusiastic and fit. 'Here,' I thought to myself, 'is the result of our training, and now for some action against the enemy.' Events were to prove me optimistic.

Once they were formed up, there began a series of the longest and most boring speeches it has ever been my fate to listen to. Only the intermittent shouts of 'Death to Fascism' and 'Liberty to the People' kept me from falling asleep. McLean's speech was by far the best, for it was the shortest. I secretly hoped that an Italian aeroplane would fly over and bring the proceedings to an end, but no such luck. At long last the speeches ended and the partisans marched off, singing lustily. The best part of the day then began with a giant barbecue. The Vlachs had roasted sheep whole on spits, and eaten in a pilaf they tasted delicious; there was plenty of raki, chianti, and beer; the celebrations finished with a good deal of singing, and McLean and I joined in an Albanian folk dance. Altogether it was an excellent party, and I strongly suspected that it was all paid for by British sovereigns.

The day after this parade, the various missions left us to go to their respective areas. All missions had code names, and ours, for some strange reason, was called — and misspelt — 'Concensus'. As the head of 'Concensus' Mission, McLean was the senior BLO in Albania, and it was for him to decide, in conjunction with Cairo, where the other missions should go after they were dropped into the country.

Accordingly, Tilman was sent to the Gjirokastër area, and Field to the Valona region. These two missions set off together, for both their destinations lay to the west, while Seymour set off north to join Abas Kupi. Kemp was extremely keen to go to Kosovo, the Albanian-populated area of Yugoslavia. We were reluctant to lose his good company, so his move north was delayed under various pretexts.

The *Shtab* came to our HQ on a number of occasions, with reports of gallant actions by the *çetas*, claiming vast numbers of Italians killed, inevitably followed by requests for more arms, combined with complaints against the Balli Kombëtar and ourselves. We desperately wanted identifications from enemy casualties, such as documents or uniform insignia taken off the bodies or prisoners. Never once did we receive any, which naturally made us suspicious of their claims.

Only on one occasion were some Italian prisoners taken; this unusual event was announced with great pride by the *Shtab*, and I was invited to go to see them for myself. I went to a house in Vithkuq where I found four Italian officers and four other ranks. They seemed resigned to their fate, for there was little doubt that they would be shot — at any rate the officers. They appeared remarkably calm and refused to give any information other than their names and the addresses of their families in Italy; I left feeling rather melancholy, for the shooting of prisoners was repugnant to me. Refusal to take prisoners in action was a different matter — the Italians had once threatened to shoot ten Albanian hostages for every Italian prisoner taken, which in itself was not an encouragement to mercy. In guerrilla warfare a prisoner is a handicap, for he has to be fed and guarded against escape; therefore, the obvious policy was not to take them. Guerrillas normally expected to be shot on the spot or executed, possibly after torture, so the system of taking no prisoners became an established feature in guerrilla warfare.

There was a further cause of dispute between ourselves and the *Shtab*. Now that the 1st Partisan Brigade was trained and equipped, why had it not been in action? After considerable eloquence on the part of McLean, combined with hints that further supplies of arms would be dependent on results, Mehmet Shehu agreed that he would carry out an action with the whole brigade, promising that some of us could accompany them to see the results for ourselves.

A few days later McLean, Kemp, and I left for the Barmash area, where the ambush was to be laid near the scene of my operation with the Ballists. After a ten hour march we found Shehu, and later in the evening we heard a few shots. That night little happened, and we assumed the partisans were all taking up their various ambush positions, so that by dawn all would be ready for the first German column. We were wrong, for early in the morning Shehu came to inform us that the operation was off. Astounded and furious, we asked him why. 'My first action must be 100 per cent successful,' replied Shehu, 'and the Germans have a post overlooking the road.' 'How many men are there in it?' we asked. 'I don't know — but about twenty,' he replied. 'Do you mean to tell me,' exclaimed McLean, 'that eight hundred partisans cannot attack and wipe out a post of twenty Germans?' Shehu, however, sullenly refused to cancel his orders. We spent almost the entire day trying to get him to change his mind, using both pleas and threats, but he was adamant, and we finally gave up in disgust at the thought that after all our training the entire partisan brigade of eight hundred men would not take on a platoon of eighteen Germans, which is what the strength of the post turned out to be.

At the time, we attributed this fiasco to rank cowardice. In fairness to Shehu, however, who was a brave man, and to the partisans themselves, we did not then know that Shehu had received a directive ordering him not to fight the Germans or Italians, but to preserve his brigade in readiness for fights with their political opponents that lay ahead.

I returned to Shtyllë to receive more supply drops, but McLean and Kemp, thirsting for action, went down to the main road alone, and successfully ambushed a German staff car, killing the occupants.

A few mornings later — on 26 August — McLean and I were sitting at the table in our living room when there was a violent explosion. All the windows were shattered, and most of the plaster from the ceiling fell on our heads. This proved to be the opening round, and a remarkably accurate one at that, of an Italian punitive expedition against Vithkuq and Shtyllë, no doubt launched in the hope of capturing us as well as dispersing the partisans.

Shells fell spasmodically in the village and around our HQ for most of the day, and for much of the time an Italian fighter circled overhead spotting; I fired a number of shots at it with the Breda, but with little effect. The partisans were conspicuous by their absence, but the villagers had already started to leave their homes and take to the woods behind Shtyllë. A stream of them could be seen carrying their most precious possessions in bundles and driving their overloaded mules before them. From the number of near misses that straddled it, our HQ became distinctly unhealthy. We decided to remove ourselves to the 'barracks' which, though nearby, was sheltered from artillery fire by virtue of its position in the lee of the mountain between it and Vithkuq. On arriving there, we made plans for evacuation should the Italians come. With the help of Duffy, Jones and Jenkins, we moved sixty canisters of explosives and ammunition to a place in the woods a couple of hundred yards away from the 'barracks', camouflaging them with green parachutes in the hope that they would not be found. They comprised the main bulk of our stores which we could not move for lack of mules. The few we had were required to carry the more essential stores such as our wireless sets and batteries.

Later in the morning, as the shelling became heavier, we saw an inspiring sight in the form of Colonel Osman Gazepi in full uniform riding a horse, escorted by his two daughters in partisan dress and carrying rifles. He appeared quite unconcerned by the shells falling around him, and as he approached us I thought he was going to be killed, for a shell burst about five yards from him and he disappeared in a cloud of smoke and dust, only to re-emerge smiling happily. His horse was also unscathed. He exchanged compliments with us and passed on his way; I never saw him again.

In the evening we decided that, in view of the complete lack of information or any word from the *Shtab* or from Shehu, various members of the mission should go out and try to discover what was happening; so McLean and Fred Nosi set off for Vithkuq, Kemp went to find Shehu, and Duffy and Jenkins started down the road to Vithkuq to lay mines; I was to stay at our HQ with the wireless operators.

It was an anxious night, and the next day brought the first signs of partisans, and they were unquestionably in full retreat. Those who passed by told me that the Italians had entered Vithkuq, and this was confirmed shortly after by McLean who returned with Fred Nosi; both had had a narrow escape when they came round a corner in Vithkuq and found themselves face to face with some Italian soldiers and were nearly captured. Kemp returned with the news that he had made contact with Shehu, who had already given the partisans orders to withdraw. Vithkuq and Shtyllë were both perfect defensive positions and would have required little effort to hold up the Italians, but Kemp reported that the partisans seemed to be completely demoralized by the bombing and shelling. We know now that Shehu had his own reasons for withdrawing the brigade.

While we packed and loaded our mules, two wounded men were brought into the barracks, as they had some sort of faith in our ability as doctors. The first was an old man whose leg had been blown off below the knee by a mortar bomb. He appeared remarkably cheerful in spite of his injuries and was delighted when we gave him a drink of raki. He soon lost consciousness and died a few hours later. The second was a young partisan of the student type who had been shot in the stomach and was evidently in great pain, making an awful noise, and crying in his agony, 'Ujë, ujë' (water, water). In my first aid training it had been impressed on me that on no account should water be given to anyone with a stomach wound, and I refused to give him any. His cries persisted, and indeed increased, and his companions evidently regarded me as needlessly cruel, so I finally relented and gave him a glass of water. He seemed greatly relieved — and so was I, for within five minutes he was dead.

We buried them quickly in indecorously shallow graves. When we heard that the Italians were near at hand, McLean told Kemp and me to take our mules, which were already loaded, into the woods behind Shtyllë to await further orders from him; this we did while shells fell uncomfortably close. Meanwhile, McLean and Fred Nosi stayed behind to see what happened.

Kemp and I spent the night in the woods, where our greatest problem was to prevent the Vlach mulemen from deserting with the mules; for as the sounds of battle drew closer, they became increasingly anxious to leave. In the morning, I returned to the 'barracks' and met McLean; he told me that the Italians had taken Vithkuq against little or no resistance from the partisans, who had moved off, so there was nobody now between us and the Italians. Shells and mortar bombs were falling more frequently, and Duffy and Jenkins arrived at this moment, having had a very narrow escape when the Italians had surprised them as they were laying mines on the road. Jenkins proudly showed us his pay book and shirt, both of which had holes from a bullet that in some extraordinary way had gone through them without touching him, for his pay book had been in his breast pocket.

McLean now ordered us to move to Panarit, a village some way off in the mountains, so I made a final tour of our HQ and 'barracks'. Since they had already been looted by the locals or partisans, nothing of value remained. We both left together — with regret, for it had been a successful and happy base — and as we looked back later we saw smoke rising from Shtyllë, and we knew that the Italians had arrived at last.

The whole mission was to reassemble at Panarit; McLean and I were the first to arrive. The rest of our party, with the mules and all our supplies intact, got there a few hours later. Here we held a conference, at which our disgust with the partisans for their showing predominated — but we still did not know that Shehu was deliberately refraining from using the partisans. It was not until later on that we had proof of this, in the form of original documents from the LNÇ Central Council that came into our hands through Professor Abas Ermenji, a Ballist leader.

We decided to split up into three parties: the main party, including Duffy, Williamson, Jones, and one wireless set would stay at Panarit; McLean and Kemp would go south to try to persuade the Ballists to attack the road, and then return to Panarit. We had now given up hope of any action by the partisans. I was to take Jenkins and Bell and his wireless set, and travel north to the Mokër region — an area lying on the western shore of Lake Ohrid, in the centre of which the frontiers of Greece, Yugoslavia and Albania all met — to reconnoitre for a new base and DZ for 'Concensus' Mission. Before moving we returned for a final look around Shtyllë, especially to see if we could recover the explosives that we had left behind. Luckily we found they had not been touched, so we recovered the lot. Of poor Shtyllë little remained except ruins, some of which were still smoking; the 'barracks' had been reduced to ashes.

We had a leisurely ride for three days, passing Voskopojë, where we found Vinçani's partisans singing songs in praise of their bravery — one would have thought that they had won a great victory. We passed through quickly, for we had no desire to dally with people from whom we could barely conceal our contempt. We later discovered that their total casualties in the entire action had been two killed and three wounded. We moved on, passing some most lovely country with steep wooded mountains, and blue rivers running through deep gorges. The villages we passed appeared more prosperous and the land, mostly laid out in terraces, more fertile. There was an abundance of plums, pears and apples on the trees, and excellent honey.

In our party we now had an interpreter we called Tom, an old rogue who had spent much of his life in America and was a born scrounger. He had an 'Old Bill' moustache, and though he wore partisan uniform with a red star in his hat, this was more for convenience than from any strong political feelings. He spoke bad English with such a peculiar American accent that at times he was quite unintelligible; but he served us well during the journey, for he appeared to have a cousin in every village we approached. This solved our problem of finding food and shelter, but in return the cousin, prompted by Tom, always seemed to want a new pair of boots, or a new battledress, or some pieces of parachute, all of which Tom knew we were carrying. At the end of the third day we reached a monastery inhabited by a monk, who was noted for his activity against the Italians. The monastery of Santa Maria lay in a very lonely part of the mountains, away from the main roads and quite inaccessible except by a steep mule track; it was also some distance from Llëngë, the nearest village.

The bearded monk, wearing a bandolier over his habit, welcomed us warmly. He seemed really pleased to see us and at once offered us coffee. He had a small *çeta* of partisans living with him in the monastery, which otherwise appeared empty, and I suggested that we should join him and make the monastery our base. At first he demurred, especially as I asked for a fair number of rooms, but Tom told us that really the only problem was that he would like some payment. After negotiations, at which no doubt Tom took his cut, he agreed to take us, but demanded a sovereign a week for each room the mission occupied; to this I agreed. We clinched the deal over some glasses of raki, with which he seemed well provided; later we found he had a liking for alcohol, and after a few drinks would indulge in practice with his rifle, shooting out of the window at anything that took his fancy, including chickens.

The monastery was ideal for an HQ. Apart from its isolation we had an excellent DZ about a mile away, and nearby a number of caves in which we could hide our stores after a drop. The one drawback was that if an enemy came down the single track leading to it, the only escape was down a precipitous track that descended into the river below us, quite impassable for mules, which would have to be abandoned in an emergency. Shortly after our arrival Bell made contact with Cairo, who gave us the news that negotiations were taking place with the Italians with a view to their capitulation. I was ordered to position myself close to the nearest Italian garrison and wait for further orders. Before a day had passed, we heard news of the Italian surrender to the Allies. Together with the monk, we all celebrated with four bottles of his champagne. I started off with Tom for Pogradec, on Lake Ohrid, where the nearest Italian garrison was located.

We took a day getting there. We found a house belonging to another friend of Tom's, where I wrote a letter to the Italian commandant, asking for a meeting. I persuaded Tom to remove the red star from his cap, and he took the letter. Shortly afterwards a number of very frightened Albanian officials appeared, for my presence was getting known. They had obviously been collaborating with the Italians, and were working hard to ingratiate themselves with me, knowing full well that the partisans were outside the town waiting for the Italians to go, when there would be little chance of their survival. They brought a rumour that the Germans were on their way to Pogradec; various other rumours were flying around when Tom returned with a reply from the Italian commandant asking me to meet him secretly in a private house.

Having smartened myself up as much as possible, to look like a British officer, and putting on my Blues forage cap in place of the white Albanian fez that I usually wore, I marched down the street with Tom, subjected to the stares of everyone we passed. Inside the house I found a colonel, a major and a captain waiting. All spoke French, so we were able to converse without an interpreter, for which I was thankful. The colonel seemed to be quite bewildered by the sudden turn of events and obviously did not know what to do, nor could he make up his mind. Pleading that he had received no orders from his superiors in Korçë, he asked me to return the next day. I was quite relieved, for I too had received no directive from Cairo and was not sure what the official line was to be.

News of the arrival of a British officer had evidently spread. I found a large crowd outside the house, and though the colonel had given me the captain as escort in case I met any Italian soldiers, my progress was impeded by the local populace. They cheered and clapped me and, to my embarrassment, old women and young girls would keep kissing me and giving me bunches of flowers — so many, in fact, that Tom had to carry them. After sending back a courier with a signal for Bell to send to Cairo explaining the situation, Tom and I, joined by some partisans, spent the night in a shepherd's hut in the hills overlooking Pogradec. We had a type of salmon-trout for our supper which tasted delicious, for one of the partisans had been down to Lake Ohrid and used a grenade to good effect.

Next morning, I re-entered the town, openly this time. The partisans were already in the town, strolling about as if they owned it, while the Italians had prudently confined themselves to barracks. To the surprise of the sentry on the gate, I walked up to the barracks and asked to be conducted to the commandant. On arriving at what I took to be the officers' mess, I found things in a state of considerable excitement. Following the colonel into a small anteroom, I spent the best part of four hours trying to persuade him and different members of his staff to bring his regiment over to join the partisans or, failing that, to hand over his arms to them. While these discussions went on, an orderly would enter at intervals with an uncooked egg on a plate, which the colonel would then crack on the table in front of him and break into his mouth, handing back the shell to the orderly — a performance that greatly intrigued me.

Now and then the colonel would go into the big room next door, where most of his officers were assembled. He would then harangue them, after which a furious discussion would break out, in which they all shouted at each other and at the colonel. From one of the staff officers I gathered that the officers themselves were very divided, some wanting to join the partisans, others the Germans, while the majority simply wanted to pack up and go back to Italy. At one stage the pro-German element seemed to be winning, for some officers with drawn pistols suddenly came into the room where I was sitting, made me hand over my own pistol and, pushing me roughly ahead of them, forced me into a room with barred windows, and locked the door. This was a very unexpected and alarming turn of events, and I was pondering on my next move when, a few minutes later, the door opened and a staff officer appeared, apologized for what he said had been a big mistake, and gave my pistol back.

The colonel then asked me if I would like to speak on the telephone to General Toriani, who commanded the Italian division based on Korçë. I said I would, but had little hope of doing so, for I thought that the partisans were sure to have cut the wires. To my surprise, the colonel returned to say that the general was on the line. I introduced myself in French, saying that I was a British officer, to which he replied that there was nothing that he could say to me as the room from which he was speaking was full of Germans; he then rang off.

I enjoyed a very good lunch in the officers' mess, sitting next to the colonel, who still went on swallowing raw eggs; afterwards, I resumed my talks with him. They ended inconclusively, because the colonel said they did not want to join the partisans. Furthermore, they were reluctant to hand their arms over to them because, he said, they would all be murdered if they did. The best I could do was to extract an assurance from him that he would not hand any of his weapons over to the Germans. With this I left, realizing that I could do no more. Collecting Tom, who had been waiting outside, I started back for Llëngë, hoping that by now some directive might have come through from Cairo.

As I left I heard firing; it appeared that the partisans were shooting at the Italians in their barracks, and I saw mortar bombs falling in the area. I met some partisans on the outskirts of the town, who told me that a carload of Germans from Korçë had driven into a partisan roadblock, and that three had been killed and four taken prisoner. I later heard the fate of these Germans from a partisan who had been present. They had been taken into a wood for execution, lined up and told to remove their boots. As they did so the partisans opened up on them with their Sten guns, but their shooting was so bad that the prisoners had picked up stones and thrown them at the partisans. The Germans were eventually killed, although one managed to run away, only to be caught and shot too. A few days later I was taken to a wood and shown their bodies, for as usual the partisans had failed to bring me any identifications. They still had their pay books in their pockets, and I had the unpleasant job of removing them. The smell was awful.

I watched the partisan operations from the hillside for some time, and saw the Italians make a sortie from their barracks; at this the partisans ran away and the Italians set a number of houses on fire, before setting fire to their own barracks. I watched them loading equipment into their transport, and as I moved off I saw lorries being driven out of the barracks. Later I heard that they had dumped their 75 mm guns in the lake, but whether to prevent them falling into German or into partisan hands I do not know; the latter is more likely. They were ambushed on their way back to Korçë. There were some casualties, but even greater numbers deserted to the partisans.

On 11 September I arrived back at Llëngë, where I found McLean. After exchanging news we decided to cut the road from the north leading to Pogradec, to prevent the Germans going to Korçë, for this was one of the very few roads in the country running north to south, and it was the main road from the garrison at Elbasan. I took a Zogist *çeta* with me whose commander, Nuri Hudinishti, I found most friendly and cooperative after my dealings with the partisans. It was one of the few operations I carried out that went according to plan. I made a number of holes in the road, using beehive charges, and filled them with 25-pound tins of ammonal, and the resulting explosion blew the whole road away from the hillside into the lake below. I had been told there was a chrome mine a few hours away, which was one of our most important economic targets in Albania. We went there but, on finding nobody working, contented ourselves with smashing the machinery. We returned to Llëngë, a day's march away.

For the next ten days I remained at Llëngë, waiting for supplies to be dropped. We received seven in all, one of which is noteworthy because the Halifax flew so low that none of the parachutes had time to open, and a large quantity of stores was destroyed, including one container of explosives that blew up like a bomb on hitting the ground. Another, full of sabotage devices, burst into flames.

At Llëngë our relations with all parties remained good, and we were visited by *çetas* from the Ballists, the Zogists, and the partisans, to all of whom we issued arms. We also had a number of Italian Alpini troops with us who were useful at the DZs. Most of these supply drops contained arms, and among the weapons sent were the Boyes anti-tank rifles which had become obsolete in the British army. It turned out to be a very useful guerrilla weapon, because it could be carried by a mule or two men and had a long and accurate range. It was useless for its original purpose against tanks but was very effective against soft transport like lorries and staff cars.

All through this period McLean tried to make contact with the Italian leaders, but failed because the Italian Commander-in-Chief, General Dalmazzo, and General Toriani in Korçë, both went over to the Germans. McLean did, however, make contact with some Bulgarian troops whom he found fraternizing with the partisans in the monastery of Shen Naum[11] on Lake Ohrid, on the frontier with Yugoslavia. We heard that thousands of Italians had come over to the partisans near Elbasan, and so we made plans for 'Concensus' Mission to move into this area. It was roughly in the middle of Albania, near the headquarters of the Central Council of the LNÇ, and was closer to areas where both the Ballists and Zogists were active.

---

[11] Sveti Naum in Slav.

On my last day at Llëngë, I attended the christening of two Albanian babies to whom I gathered I was godfather, which meant a handout of sovereigns to the parents. The babies were tapped smartly on the head by the priest, who used parachute cord for this purpose. He then completely immersed the naked babies in a font full of holy water. He had put on some very fine robes over his battledress and bandolier, and during the ceremony he parked his Sten gun on the pulpit.

That afternoon the Ballist *çeta* brought in three German prisoners from an ambush in which they had killed seven; this figure was confirmed by a British sergeant who had been with them. He said that one of the Albanians had scored a direct hit on a staff car with the Boyes rifle; the car had capsized and burst into flames. The Ballist leader insisted on giving me the three Germans as a present, which was an easy way out for him. They were all wounded, and the problem arose of what to do with them. The local partisans were all for shooting them on the spot, but I had other ideas. First I dressed their wounds — one had a bullet in his wrist and foot, another had a bullet that had entered his chest and gone out through his back, and the third had fragments from a grenade in his back and his behind. I then interrogated them in my halting German. They all claimed to be Austrians, two being medical orderlies and one a *feldgendarm* or military policeman. The two medical orderlies had documents to prove their statements, but the *feldgendarm* did not, and I suspected that he was lying. When the partisans again demanded to shoot them, I said that the orderlies were protected by the Red Cross. I nearly let them shoot the *feldgendarm*, but finally decided against it.

I knew that the next day we must cross a main road along which German convoys frequently passed. I therefore decided to dump our prisoners on this road, where they could be picked up, although it did involve a slight risk to ourselves. We set off, with our prisoners on mules, and when we came to the road I told them what we were going to do; they were profoundly grateful, for they had been uncertain of their fate. I told them that I would wait near the road and see them picked up, but made them promise not to point me out to their friends. I sent the mules on with the rest of the party, while I waited about a hundred yards away to see what would happen. Within twenty minutes a German convoy came along, and they signalled it to stop. After a short discussion, they were all helped in. None of them made any signs until the convoy started off, when they leaned out of their windows and waved happily at me.

For three days we moved along a track overlooking the new main road to Elbasan that had been built by the Italians. We were very close to the main road at times, and saw plenty of German transport and, at two places, German-occupied barracks. We felt fairly secure, however, because the Shkumbin river flowed between the main road and our track — though we were well in range if anyone had cared to shoot at us. At one place we passed there were some large fortifications tunnelled into the mountainside; we entered them to find an Albanian inside, who warned us that they were in use, and that the Germans had been there that morning. A road led away from these fortifications and we moved down it by night until we reached the Shkumbin river, which we crossed by a large wooden bridge. I was with a small partisan *çeta* at the time, and the leader suggested that as it led to the fortifications it might be worth blowing up. I heartily agreed, for I liked blowing things up. As we crossed the Shkumbin we dumped the explosives that we needed, and the mule party, after crossing the bridge, plodded on up a track on the other side of the main road. I remained at the bridge with two men to help me place the charges on the two piers. Then I sent them on to join the mules. I set fuses with a ten-minute delay in the charges to give myself time to get away, as I had been told that there were two German barracks sited about a mile from the bridge, one in either direction up and down the road.

I made a stupid mistake in setting the fuses. I initiated the charge nearest the main road first. (To initiate a charge, one squeezes the end of a time pencil, which is attached to the fuse. This breaks a glass phial in the pencil, and this releases an acid, which then eats into a wire and is supposed to break it in ten minutes; the delay depends on the thickness of the wire.) I had just initiated the second charge and was about to walk back the hundred yards across the bridge, when to my horror there was a violent explosion: the first charge had gone off — after two minutes rather than ten. I threw myself on my face and was luckily unhurt by the falling debris. However, I was now on the bridge, with a gaping hole where I wanted to cross — and the charge behind me, if it was as unreliable as the first one, might go off any minute. So I ran back past it and decided my only chance was to wade across the Shkumbin, which I had been told was only about four feet deep. I was wrong again, for as I waded across, it became deeper and deeper, until finally I found myself swimming; worse still, the current was taking me down towards the bridge that was due to blow up. Almost exhausted I reached the other side, and as I was climbing the bank the second charge detonated. I lay on the ground for a moment, then climbed on to the main road, to be greeted with a burst of machine-gun fire from one direction along the road and, very shortly after, by rifle shots from the other. I sprinted across the road, and — luckily in the moonlight — found the track the mules had taken and started to climb as fast as I could. I heard men running and shouting on the road but climbed on without stopping.

I was wet through and completely out of breath; only the thought of possible pursuers kept me from throwing myself to the ground in sheer exhaustion. After about ten minutes, two figures appeared in front of me — the two partisans who had helped me on the bridge. They urged me to hurry, for they had heard the firing. I could not hurry and could hear no signs of pursuit; shooting was still going on down the road, though at what I was too exhausted to know, or care. My only wish was to lie down and sleep, but my two escorts urged me on, and we climbed for nearly eight hours before coming to a village where I could throw myself down on the floor of a house and sleep.

I had been asleep for barely two hours when one of the partisans rushed in to wake me, saying that we must move at once, because the owner of the house had gone off to warn the Germans of our presence. Although I had doubts about this it proved to be true, for though we left immediately, I saw a patrol of about a dozen German soldiers entering the bottom end of the village from the track below as we left the upper end by another. Once clear of the houses we were fully exposed on the mountainside, and the Germans must have seen us for they started to shoot at us at extreme range. Only a few spent bullets arrived anywhere near us, but they served to spur us on.

The Germans followed us up the track, pausing now and then to let off a few harmless shots at us. At one spot both sides of the track were covered with masses of delicious-looking ripe wild strawberries, and I could not resist stopping to pick and eat some. My companions ahead of me shouted at me to come on as the Germans narrowed the gap between us, so I hurried to the top of a ridge where I turned back to see how the Germans were getting on. To my delight, they too had stopped and were all picking and eating wild strawberries: at which point they must have given up the chase, for they failed to pursue us over the ridge.

In a few hours we reached Labinot, where I found Williamson with his wireless set, some of the *Shtab*, and a great number of Italian soldiers who had joined the partisans. I wanted to sleep, but in a short time Enver Hoxha stormed in in a fury and demanded to know who had given me permission to blow the bridge. I told him I did not need permission from the *Shtab* to blow a bridge, and furthermore the *çeta* leader with me had also thought it was a good idea — in fact, he had suggested it. 'He must have been a Ballist,' Hoxha snorted, and stumped away. This bridge-blowing episode must have rankled considerably with the *Shtab*, because it was brought up against me as a complaint at every subsequent meeting. When I met Brigadier 'Trotsky' Davies after the war, he told me that Enver Hoxha and Mehmet Shehu continually complained to him about this incident.

Chapter VII: Arrival of 'Trotsky's' mission and our evacuation

Three days later at Labinot I got a letter from McLean which contained the gist of a signal from Cairo. In view of the increasing numbers of British missions in Albania, it was intended to drop a more senior officer and his staff to take over from 'Concensus' HQ the command and organization of all these missions. McLean added that the *Shtab* had told him of a possible DZ at Biza. He wanted me to go there and, if I found it suitable, to set up a base there for the new party when it arrived.

I left Labinot, passing a large camp in the mountains containing hundreds of Italian soldiers, and arrived at Biza on 10 October 1943. On arrival, I was very pleased to find a long though narrow grassy plain about two miles long and half a mile across, situated in a hollow with mountains rising on either side. It was on a high plateau which dropped down to foothills leading to the Tirana plain on the west, the east end rising through large beech forests. It was an ideal place for a base, and, for security, I sited the HQ on the edge of the forest, where a shepherd's wooden hut already stood. Because we needed considerably more room than the one hut, I arranged for a number of Italian soldiers to be sent to help in building the new accommodation. They had few tools but were good improvisers. They built a number of huts, some as living quarters, some as sleeping quarters, and smaller ones as stores or for a kitchen. Branches of beech trees formed the sides, and green camouflaged parachutes made up the roofs.

While this building was taking place, I went to see the local *çeta* leader. I wanted to make arrangements to get early warning of the approach of any enemy from his direction. His village was some miles away, on the only mule track that led to the rear of our position. I was particularly interested to meet this man, for he was the same Baba Faja whose name, together with those of Myslim Pesa and Abas Kupi, had been originally mentioned in Cairo by Mrs Hasluck.

His real name was Baba Mustafa, though he was always known as Baba Faja. A priest or *hoj* of the Bektashi sect, his monastery at Martenesh had been burnt down some time before by the Italians. He was a well-built and rather stout man, with a massive black beard. Apart from his priest's hat, which he always wore, his usual dress was a loud check plus-four suit over which he slung his bandolier and pistol. He was a likeable character, but a scoundrel, and he drank heavily. (Bektashis are in fact permitted to drink alcohol, unlike the other Moslem sects.) He delighted in singing partisan songs in his deep bass voice, especially after consuming large quantities of raki. We did not take long to discover that he was being used as a figurehead by the partisans, and always had a commissar at his elbow to keep an eye on him.

He promised to help and showed great interest when I said I might need the help of his men for drops of arms and supplies. From then on Baba Faja was an unmitigated nuisance, turning up at every supply drop and begging for arms, equipment, or food. I always had to give him something to get rid of him, but finally I foisted him onto Kadri Hoxha, the commissar for the local partisan brigade, to whom I issued all supplies on signature, after which I could refer Baba Faja to him for all requests.

On my return to Biza I found that McLean had arrived from a visit to Myslim Pesa, where he had taken part in a hard-fought action against the Germans. He said that the Italians who had deserted to Myslim Pesa had given a good account of themselves, and though they had suffered heavy casualties, McLean had counted a good many German dead.

To make our HQ more habitable for the new party, we enlisted some camp followers from among the Italians, including cooks, waiters, a barber, a tailor, a shoemaker, and an armourer. By the time the new party was due to drop the HQ was ready, and the signal fires were laid. Since the bombing of our DZ at Shtyllë, we had devised a new system of signalling. The big recognition fires, from six to ten in number, were now lit about two miles away from the DZ by some of our retainers, under the command of one of our NCOs; these were the normal wood bonfires. The real DZ was prepared at a certain bearing from the fires only known to us and the pilots, and there we placed two or three bully-beef tins filled with earth and soaked with petrol. On hearing the engines of the aircraft we simply put a match to the tins, and the aircraft dropped their supplies on these fires; we were easily able to extinguish our tins, and if any enemy aircraft came it would probably drop its bombs on the decoy DZ.

The day arrived when the new party was due. We sat up all night, but nothing came; the same happened the next night. It was very cold, for we were at an altitude of nearly 3000 feet. The sorties were not usually expected much before midnight, and we normally waited until about three o'clock; after that it was unlikely that the Halifaxes would come, because they liked to be clear of the enemy fighters based on Greece before first light. If nothing came by three we would pack up and return, cold and dispirited, to our sleeping quarters.

At about eight o'clock on the third night, I was in our hut having dinner before setting out for the DZ. As I was sipping a mug of German beer, I heard engines. No fires had been lit and so, sending off a Verey light into the sky to attract the aircraft's attention, we signalled at it with a torch to wait while we lit the fires. They were a quarter of an hour's walk away, but we ran all the way and eventually got them alight. The drop was a success. The first party of officers and NCOs to land were led by Brigadier 'Trotsky' Davies, and included Lieutenant-Colonel Arthur Nicholls, his GI,[12] Major Jim Chesshire, his Sapper expert, and Major Alan Palmer; from a following aircraft more were successfully dropped, including Captain Alan Hare as Staff Captain, Captain Trayhorn as Signals officer, Captain Victor Smith, and a Pole called Captain Michael Lis. We were flabbergasted by the amount of kit they brought, which included a quantity of camp furniture and two containers of stationery; one of the new NCOs was a clerk, complete with typewriter.

Palmer and Smith left the next day to join the Partisan Brigade in the south, and Palmer eventually became the senior British officer attached to the partisans. Chesshire only stayed a short time; he was clearly a man after my own heart, whose ardent wish was to go and blow up something, so he left with this intention.

Of those who remained, the leader was Brigadier Davies, known to all Albanians as 'the General' and to us as 'Trotsky'. He had been given this nickname early in his military career, and kept it in his signals, for we all had code names for

---

[12] Staff officers who served on the staff of a Brigade or Divisional Headquarters were officially known as General Staff Officers and were graded by rank. A General Staff Officer I, abbreviated to GSOI, and further abbreviated to GI, was usually a lieutenant-colonel. A Brigade Major was a GII and a Staff Captain a GIII.

signalling purposes. McLean's was 'Paste' and mine was 'Grin'; these ghastly puns were not chosen by us.

Trotsky was considerably older than the rest of us, and much senior in rank; he had served most of his career in the Royal Ulster Rifles. With greying hair and going bald, of thickset build with a tendency to stoutness, he showed considerable courage on doing a parachute jump at his age and seniority; he had already won an MC and bar,[13] and was later awarded a DSO for his activities in Albania. He had a military moustache and a brick red face, a hearty and friendly manner, and was a very experienced regular soldier.

The next senior officer was Lieutenant-Colonel Arthur Nicholls of the Coldstream Guards. Very tall and slim, with a dark moustache, he too was much older than, and more senior to, McLean and me. He could best be described as a typical Foot Guards officer, with all the characteristics of that very special breed of soldier — wholly admirable in the regular army, but not entirely suited to guerrilla warfare.

Captain Alan Hare of the Life Guards was tall, of medium build; he usually wore glasses and looked too studious and intellectual to warrant the description of typical, either as a Household Cavalry or a regular officer. At the battle of Alamein, he had served with the Household Cavalry Regiment as Technical Adjutant, which seemed a strange appointment for him. He was very intelligent, with a strong sense of the ridiculous, and seemed somehow not to fit in with the intense military atmosphere that now prevailed; but his physical toughness and courage in adversity were later to be proved.

Captain Michael Lis was a small man with a pointed foxy face, a large drooping moustache and a cheerful grin. He had

---

[13] A silver bar worn on the ribbon of a medal indicates that it has been awarded a second time.

been sent to Albania to organize an escape route from the country for any Polish prisoners or evaders who might have escaped from the Germans. He had survived a pretty hair-raising escape from his own country and was well qualified for the job, but it turned out that there were few Poles in Albania requiring his help, and so he became attached to one of the missions as a Liaison Officer; he proved to be a considerable help, for he not only spoke French and English in addition to his native language, but was an adept scrounger — a most useful characteristic in guerrilla life.

Our first conference was presided over by Trotsky, and it was clear we were in for big changes. One of his first remarks, addressed to McLean, was, 'Well McLean, I noticed there was no stand-to this morning.' ('Stand-to' is a term used for that period when soldiers, dressed, armed, and at their posts, stand-to to repel possible enemy attacks. There are two such periods a day, the first from an hour before dawn until dawn, and the second from dusk or sunset until one hour after dusk — these two periods being when attacks are considered most likely.) Trotsky continued, 'We will start stand-to tomorrow. What time does the sun rise?' A look of horror flashed across McLean's face, for we seldom got up before eight or nine in the morning because we usually went to bed so late. With commendable skill, he smartly passed the buck. Turning to me, he said, 'What time would you say, David?' I followed the old army principle of 'give an answer, right or wrong.' 'Six o'clock,' I hazarded. 'Right,' said Trotsky, 'stand-to tomorrow morning at five o'clock.' This shook us considerably, and our NCOs Jones and Jenkins and the two wireless operators almost mutinied on the spot. The following morning, we all stood-to from five to six, and were then stood down; whereupon

McLean and I went back to bed. This was not looked upon favourably.

Later in the same conference, Trotsky told all the officers that he wanted them to dress like British officers, keep up a smart appearance, and set a good example in front of the Albanians and Italians. He did not make any comments on McLean or myself; they were presumably better left unsaid, for we had by now become very individualistic in our manner of dress. McLean usually wore jodhpurs with a large dark red cummerbund, a grey uniform shirt, and a variety of headgear; but whatever it was, he always wore the silver eagle of the Royal Scots Greys. My dress was corduroy trousers, Albanian sandals with Alpini studs in the soles, a khaki shirt, and a jersey or battledress blouse according to the weather, with a white Albanian fez.

A few days later, McLean and I were in our sleeping quarters. The walls of beech branches and the proximity of the huts made every word anyone said audible to all. We heard Nicholls reprimanding Hare. 'You're getting as untidy as those fellows McLean and Smiley,' he complained, 'and they've gone completely native.' He was probably right.

Tidiness was not a feature of our camps, for we had long since given up trying to teach our followers not to litter the ground with any rubbish they did not want, and had grown to accept debris lying around. On one of the first days, our retainers were mustered for a great clearing-up operation; Vlachs, Albanians, and Italians formed up in a line and were ordered by Nicholls to go through the camp picking up every piece of paper, old cigarette packets, tins, bottles, and the like. The Vlachs and Albanians clearly thought the British colonel was mad but had to be humoured, so shrugging their shoulders they carried out his orders. When they arrived at the other end of the camp area Nicholls expressed his pleasure and told them to fall out, whereupon to a man they threw on the ground everything they had collected; Nicholls's comments were unprintable.

McLean and I were very worried about the large size of the new HQ, which would have required over one hundred mules to move it. We feared that the new mission would not adapt itself to the true facts of irregular warfare and would develop more on military and less on guerrilla lines, which was just what we had been trying to stop the Albanian partisans from doing. Our responsibilities and worries diminished, however, when we were ordered back to Cairo to report on the situation in Albania. Trotsky told us he thought it only right that, as the first British officers to enter the country, we should also be the first to go out. We were very grateful to him for arranging this. He was very kind and considerate by nature, and probably thought a change and a rest would do us good.

We stayed at Biza for a week after the arrival of the new party, McLean briefing Trotsky and his staff on everything that he possibly could, giving his views on various personalities, warning him of the political problems that lay ahead of him, and especially of the complete unreliability of the partisans. I handed over all our supplies, mules, and retainers to Hare, warning him who were the biggest thieves and giving him other useful hints. I also handed over my mule Fanny, for whom I had formed a real affection over a period of months, and whose sad fate has already been told. We did not take mules with us because we were travelling very light, and planned to do the first part of our return journey by car. This was a novel method of travel to us in Albania, but we had already bought a new Fiat for forty sovereigns to do our shopping with; it was possible to drive across the plain to a track leading onto a new military road made by the Italians between Elbasan and Burrel. Williamson was to come with us and bring his wireless and batteries. This was our only heavy piece of equipment and would need a mule to carry it.

The whole mission including our retainers turned up to see us off, and I wondered when we would see them again. I felt many regrets at leaving them all. Jones and Jenkins were also left behind, for by now they had become almost indispensable. Our Albanian bodyguards, mulemen, and Italians looked very sad as we said goodbye. Some even wept.

There was still, however, the problem of getting out of the country, and we decided that our best chance was to be picked up off the coast south of Valona; it was not far to Italy by boat from the Albanian coast. The barren Albanian mountains that ran south to the Greek frontier dropped steeply into the sea, and there were numbers of small creeks accessible to boats; they were also far enough away from the main road and any villages to be secure from German troops. It was for this area that we were now aiming; it involved a longish march down the southern half of Albania — over a hundred miles as the crow flies — but probably more than double this by the devious routes that we should have to take.

After a two hour drive we got out, met a guide with a mule, and, after a short walk, reached Labinot, where we stayed for two days with the Central Council of the LNÇ. They knew we were leaving the country and had endless requests to make of McLean. I left him alone to deal with all these people, for he enjoyed the political side of our lives. I was not only bored stiff by politics, but I had an intense dislike of most of the members of the LNÇ Central Council. McLean, in spite of his great political differences with them, seemed somehow to retain an interest in their personalities, and even a certain respect and affection for many of them.

Enver Hoxha and Mehmet Shehu were not on speaking terms with me after the episode of the blown bridge. (Strangely enough, we crossed the road in the same place on our journey south and had to be ferried over on a pontoon.) Of the others I took a particular dislike to Seifulla Malleshova, an intellectual known as the 'Red Poet', with whom I quarrelled frequently. McLean must have saved my life several times by restraining me from coming to blows with some of them.

I was thankful to leave Labinot. We spent our next night at Llixhë, which was normally a health resort, but had been taken over as a hospital by the partisans; there we enjoyed the luxuries of bathing in hot sulphur baths, in water that came from natural hot springs, and of sleeping in beds between sheets — the first time we had done so in Albania. It was in Llixhë that we saw Italian soldiers in the town who, we were told, were for sale. We did not quite understand this at first and queried the translation, but we were assured that this was really true, and were given the following explanation; after the Italian capitulation in July 1943, their soldiers in central and southern Albania had taken to the mountains, and those who brought their arms and wished to fight the Germans joined the partisans. Those who brought no arms, or had let the Albanians remove them, became a problem, for they needed food and this was getting scarce. So they were put to work in the fields and villages, to which they had no objection because in return they received board and lodging. What we had seen was a collection of Italians waiting to be selected by the Albanians for whom they were going to work. However, any Albanian who wanted to employ an Italian had to pay for him, the usual price being a gold napoleon or sovereign, by then the only acceptable form of currency; presumably this went to the funds of the LNÇ. Considering what the Albanians had suffered under Italian rule, especially under the more recent policy of reprisals, it was surprising how tolerant and forgiving they were towards them. They professed a contempt for them, but seldom ill-treated them, though certain members of the partisan commissars committed atrocities shortly after the surrender, when a number of Italians were murdered for their arms and clothing.

Leaving Llixhë, we walked for two days until we came to a village near Berat, where we met a Balli Kombëtar outpost; they insisted on our partisan escort being left behind if we wanted to proceed, for we were entering Ballist territory. We had no choice but to agree and were then provided with a Ballist escort, which took us to meet the leader. He was Professor Abas Ermenji; I had already heard of him as the military leader of the Balli Kombëtar movement.

He was a dark, serious, intelligent, and capable man, though a trifle intense. We took a liking to him, for he proved to be co-operative and helpful, and later he led a number of successful actions against the Germans in which he distinguished himself. On the morning we met him he gave us a full account of the situation, from which he correctly drew the conclusion that civil war was imminent. Among other things, he showed us a document that his *çetas* had captured from the partisans. This document, dated 9 September 1943, was a circular letter from the LNÇ Central Council to all regional committees. It was so revealing that we made notes and translations from it; the following are extracts:

> In case of an Allied landing the National Liberation Councils must be the real power. They must mobilize the whole people round them and should not allow

other forces such as the Balli Kombëtar to exert any influence on the people... The National Liberation forces must begin from now on to assert themselves everywhere, and, when the landing takes place, they must present themselves to the Allies, through the National Liberation Councils as the only power of the Albanian people... The administration of Albania should be entirely in the hands of the Liberation Councils.

This was clearly the explanation for the reluctance of Mehmet Shehu to commit the 1st Partisan Brigade into any action against the Germans, and was written proof, if further proof was necessary, that the LNÇ had no intention of keeping the Mukaj Agreement.

This agreement came about in the following way. At the time of the Italian surrender in July 1943, a meeting was held in the house of Ihsan Bey Toptani at Topize. Toptani was a patriotic Albanian from a distinguished family, whose father had been a member of the first Albanian Regency Council after Albania became independent. He was not aligned with any particular political party and was in touch with the leaders of all parties, and so his house was a suitable neutral ground where they could all meet. However, the Italians got wind of the meeting and sent out troops and tanks to arrest those taking part, and the whole meeting had to be transferred to the village of Mukaj.

At the meeting the leaders of the LNÇ, including Abas Kupi, for at this time the LNÇ in theory was formed as a broad nationalist front, and the Balli Kombëtar all came to an understanding. On 2 August they signed an agreement, the most important points of which were: firstly, the setting up of a committee of twelve members (six from the LNÇ and six from the Balli Kombëtar), called 'The Committee for the Salvation of Albania'; secondly, both parties agreed that they would fight against the German and Italian occupiers of their country until Albania was free; and thirdly, they agreed that after liberation the form of the regime would be determined by the people of Albania. This agreement was almost immediately denounced by the Central Council of the LNÇ. It was this action that caused Abas Kupi to leave the LNÇ in disgust and reactivate his own party, known as the Legality Movement, which became more commonly known as the Zogist Movement.

Passing through Ballist outposts, we again entered partisan-held territory, and reached the recently liberated town of Berat. An old citadel on a great rock dominated the picturesque houses of the town. It was full of partisans and Italians milling around, apparently oblivious to the proximity of the German troops who were gathering on the outskirts of the town. We stayed an uneasy two days there, sleeping in the biggest hotel, on whose front door was a sign in Albanian saying 'Commissars only'; thus honoured, we were able to appreciate the hot baths that were available. We had friends in the town, Gjin Marku, Kahreman Ylli, and Captain Islam Radovicka, who helped us and who gave us much information about the Germans, with whom they accused the Balli Kombëtar of collaborating. They procured us mules, and an ex-Italian army horse for me to ride, and sent us on our way with a partisan escort. Two days later, the Germans occupied Berat without opposition.

We passed a partisan outpost on the outskirts of the town; a mile further on we came upon a Ballist patrol, and again we had to dispense with our partisan escort, but thanks to our letter from Abas Ermenji we were allowed to proceed. We had to show this letter to two more patrols who stopped us, and it proved a most useful *laissez passer*.

We climbed for some hours over a high range of mountains. My horse was very unsure of itself on the mountain tracks, continually slipping and stumbling, until finally it slipped and fell over the edge of the track. I was riding at the time but managed to slip my feet out of the stirrups and throw myself off as the unfortunate animal fell over a sheer drop of over a hundred feet and was killed. I determined never to ride a horse in the mountains again, for the mules were uncannily surefooted, and Fanny never gave me a fall in all the months I rode her.

When we reached the lower slopes of the mountains we entered the village of Shepër, where Tilman had his HQ. He had made himself very comfortable and entertained us lavishly, but told us a gloomy story of his relations with the partisans, for whom he obviously had little love. He complained that in his area, which included Gjirokastër and its German garrison, he could get no co-operation from any of the partisans in any actions against the Germans. The only fighting in his area, he added, was between the partisans and the Ballists, while the Germans were left alone. He consoled himself by keeping fit; climbing Mount Nemërcka, the range we had just crossed, was very convenient for this purpose.

We stayed for three days at Tilman's HQ, during which time we made contact with Cairo; they gave us the good news that a boat would be coming to evacuate us in ten days' time, but told us that we must find a suitable point on the coast from which we could be picked up, and then send them the fullest details for the Navy. We decided that I should set off immediately, for time was short; travelling light without a mule, I would take a guide and reconnoitre the coast until I found a suitable point.

Once this was done I was to make for Field's HQ in the Valona area, and McLean would come on with Williamson and the wireless set as soon as he had hired some mules — for those we had brought from Berat had got to return there.

Mules were becoming a problem in this area; there was a grave shortage because the thousands of Italians in the mountains, who were running short of food, had already eaten all their horses and were now turning to eating mules.

It took me three days to reach the coast, crossing the Gjirokastër valley; during this trip I passed villages full of Italians in the last stages of starvation, some simply lying at the sides of tracks dying. On the second day I came to a village in which I found Bedri Spahiu, the commissar who had given us such a bad reception on our first entry into Albania. I found him in the only house in the village that had not been burnt down by the Germans three weeks previously; this time, he was more co-operative and produced a local partisan guide who knew the coast. He had a number of partisans with him, but the whole atmosphere was one of gloom, for apart from the ruined village, groups of half-starved Italians and skinny mules were standing around dejectedly and some, both Italians and mules, had collapsed on the ground, and were unlikely to get up alive. At least the mules could be eaten, and from now on whenever I was given meat I suspected it was mule.

Near the coast I came to a village where there were some Italians, and as I was staying the night I joined them; they were pleading with me to get them a boat to take them back to Italy, and said that a boat had already been over but had only taken away senior officers. They asked me to join them for their only meal of the day; I accepted, for I was travelling light and had no food of my own. We had a sort of stew, well laced with pepper or some similar hot spice; I thought one or two of them were eyeing me suspiciously as I ate, and afterwards they asked me if I had enjoyed it. I said 'Yes, I suppose it was mule,' to which one of them replied, 'No, it was an Italian.' They assured me that they were in such a state of starvation in the area that as men died off, some of their comrades were eating their flesh. Whether this was true remains in doubt.

The first beach I saw was unsuitable; after swimming out to test its gradient and depth I found it was too shallow, and it was too near to a road that was used by the Germans. The sea was very cold, and the walk back to the village of Borsh warmed me up, as did some raki on my arrival. There I had a further delay, for the villagers insisted on showing me the graves of sixty-five Italian officers whom the Germans had forced them to bury. They saw them killed by the Germans, who, they said, tied the Italians' hands, lined them up, shot them down with machine-guns, and finished off the wounded with bayonets. They were clearly very frightened of the Germans after what they had seen, and seemed relieved to see me go. I made for a village where we had heard there was a British officer, but instead of finding Field, as I had expected, I found McLean. He had received a signal from Cairo giving the position of Field's HQ, which was not very far away, and so we set off together. We passed two villages in flames — not German reprisals this time, but the partisans burning down Ballist villages; the civil war had started in earnest. Passing through another village full of listless starving Italians, we reached Field's HQ, situated in a dilapidated shack on the top of a mountain. Field was not there, but we were greeted by his British NCO and a group of Italians. It was bitterly cold, for it was now November, and they seemed very short of food. The British corporal told us that Field had fallen out with both partisans and Ballists, and was so disgusted with both factions that he would have nothing to do with either; he refused to have an Albanian near him, and had surrounded himself with Italians.

There was a note from Field to say that he had left to reconnoitre a place on the coast which he had heard might be suitable for our evacuation, and so we decided to join him. The day before I reached the coast, I passed the burnt-out wreckage of a Halifax. Field told me an amazing story about it. It had been bringing him a new officer and supplies and had made a trial run over the dropping ground. As it came over a second time, it suddenly nosedived into the mountain. All the occupants except the rear gunner, ten in all, were killed. The rear gunner had a miraculous escape for, on hitting the ground the tail section had broken off and he was thrown clear, knocked unconscious, but received no injuries other than a few scratches. When he came round, he found that a partisan had removed and stolen his boots. Field added that the partisans had behaved very badly, looted everything, and had even refused to bury the dead; luckily he had some Italians to help him in this gruesome task.

We met a guide from Field, who led us across the Valona-Himarë road in daylight; it did not seem to be used very much by the Germans and we only saw a few lone military vehicles, although we noticed that the Germans were also using civilian lorries. Climbing the high mountain of Dukat, we crossed over the summit, from which we had some magnificent views of the Adriatic, and descended a steep track towards the sea; before dark we found Field and some Italians, who had established themselves in a cave in the cliffs.

Field confirmed what had been told us about his attitude towards the Albanians and the Italians. He still hoped to take action with the Italians against the Germans, providing he was sent enough food for them. He said they had already been useful in producing intelligence from Valona, and one of his officers, a Captain Munzetti, who had previously been the Italian Intelligence Officer in Valona, had been especially useful. Later we met Munzetti and found him a brave and efficient officer. At great personal risk of being recognized, he used to go into Valona in civilian clothes and carry out various assignments for Field.

We spent a week in this cave, which was long and very low; having previously sheltered sheep and goats, it was riddled with lice. We kept in touch with Cairo, but their signals filled us with despair, for they brought us nothing but news of postponements of the boat, for reasons that seemed to us quite groundless. We were desperately keen to go, for we were very rapidly running out of food and water. The mule that had carried the wireless set died, and for the week that we were there this was the only meat we ate, eked out one day by some tinned food that Munzetti had bought in Valona. There was no water locally, and we would have run out but for a very fortunate storm one night; after that, our only meagre supply was what we could collect from puddles in the rocks with a sponge.

This was the only time throughout the war when I felt real pangs of hunger. It was ironic that at this moment we received a signal from Cairo in reply to one we had sent from Biza, where McLean and I had discovered that we were suffering from worms. We had asked what we should do to treat this unpleasant complaint. The signal we received started, 'Treatment for worms. One. Starve for twenty-four hours…' By my reckoning, we had already complied with this part of the treatment!

One day we had a good view from the cliffs of a German hospital ship steaming past, and on another evening we had a grandstand view of a naval action, when we saw two of our own destroyers racing past with all guns firing. They were so close that we could hear the throb of their engines and the orders transmitted on the loudspeakers; shortly afterwards, we saw a ship in flames on the horizon. After our return to Bari, we discovered that a German tanker and two escorting F-boats had been sunk in this action.

Our resentment with our base in Cairo increased, as our shortage of food and water became more acute. The last straw was when a local peasant appeared, claiming to be the owner of the cave in which we were living, and said that unless we paid him a rent of a sovereign a day he would inform the Germans of our presence. We paid, but looking back I wonder why we did not shoot him and dump him in the sea.

Our evacuation point was a dog-legged creek about a hundred yards in length, with steep cliffs up both sides but with a small beach about five yards long at the shore end. It already had the code name of 'Seaview', and it was ideal for its purpose providing the sea remained calm; in rough weather it was impossible, and for two days following a storm there was a considerable swell. Extending to the sea at one side of the entrance to 'Seaview' was a rocky promontory, and for the last two nights, on both of which a boat was due, I sat on this promontory flashing the letter 'K' seawards, this being the agreed recognition signal. At about midnight on the second night, I heard engines and received answering flashes to mine; to my relief, our friends had at last arrived. After some time, we saw a small boat approaching, in which two men were seated; we shouted to them to paddle up to the beach, for they were dangerously near the rocks and quite a swell was running.

On landing, the two men jumped out; one was a naval officer who introduced himself as Sandy Glen, and the other was an American officer whose name I did not hear, but I was told later he was from the OSS (Office of Strategic Services, the American counterpart of SOE).

Both officers said that they had come to stay, and we were delighted to see them; but our pleasure was considerably dampened when they told us that the boat, which was of the collapsible rubber type, had a large hole in its bottom and was leaking so badly that it could not possibly get us back to the MTB. McLean and I were determined to go, even if it meant swimming out to the boat; but each of us had a briefcase of documents, German maps, and other items of interest to Cairo. I had, in addition, several rolls of films for developing, and my diary. We therefore decided to block the hole in the boat with a blanket and try to reach the MTB.

Shaking hands with numerous people who had come down to see us off, we were successfully launched against the swell. While I rowed as hard as I could, McLean bailed furiously. It was proving to be a losing battle, for the boat was clearly filling with water quicker than McLean could bail; but we were now nearing the MTB. We reached it and flung our briefcases up onto the deck just as the small boat sank; McLean and I were only swimming for a matter of seconds before helping hands dragged us out of the water. We were hauled aboard to find that the officer in command of the boat was an old acquaintance, Lieutenant David Scott.

Scott said he had some cases of food for Field's mission, but since the rubber boat had now sunk he would not be able to get them to him. We explained Field's desperate circumstances, and so Scott moved his boat in to the promontory in spite of the risk of the heavy swell; when the MTB was almost touching the rocks, the sailors hurled the boxes of bully beef ashore, while Field's Italians grabbed them before they fell into the sea or were swept away. All this time I was violently seasick, but as soon as we were under way we were plied with stiff drinks while we dried off.

I left the coast of Albania with few regrets, and as the mountains receded in the distance my spirits rose. After an uneventful three hour crossing of the Adriatic we reached Brindisi, had a good breakfast on board, then cruised up the coast to Bari and entered the harbour. We were first taken aboard HMS *Forth*, a depot ship for submarines and MTBs, where we had a welcome bath and shave, followed by pink gins and an excellent lunch — at least it tasted excellent after our recent meals in Albania.

We were collected from the depot ship by a conducting officer from the SOE office in Bari — by now the Cairo office was in the process of being transferred to Italy. He told us that before we saw anyone he was taking us to hospital to be deloused, for ever since living in the cave at 'Seaview' we had been lousy.

Wallowing in a bath of very strong carbolic, I was happy to be rid of these tiny companions; but I was furious to discover that while I was having my bath all my clothes, which I thought were being fumigated, had in fact been put into the hospital incinerator and burnt. The conducting officer had produced new battledress for us. I suppose he was only doing his best, but he could not have known that not only was I very attached to my corduroy trousers, but they had been especially doctored before going into Albania with escaping devices. Sewn into the waist belt were two silk maps of the Balkans and Europe; in one of the seams above a pocket was a six-inch hacksaw; the fly buttons were magnetic; and, worst of all, two sovereigns were sewn in each of the turn-ups of the trousers.

We stayed in Bari for three days. On the first day General Alexander interviewed and questioned us in his HQ north of Bari, after which he kindly invited us to stay to lunch. We spent the rest of the time visiting so many offices that I cannot remember them all, but in each we were subjected to a barrage of questions on those aspects of Albania which particularly interested them. The SOE commander in Bari told us that he was sending us back to Cairo to see the various SOE departments, including the Albanian section, which was still there, after which we would be flown to London.

We flew from Bari to Cairo, where we were met by a tall, languid officer of the Coldstream Guards, who introduced himself as Billy Moss and informed us that he was our conducting officer. There were so many people who wanted to see us, in so many offices and different organizations, that without a conducting officer we should never have found our way or arrived on time.

We found major changes in the Albanian section, for it had greatly expanded since we had left Mrs Hasluck in sole charge. In command was Major Philip Leake, a charming officer who had been a schoolmaster in civil life, but who had served as a staff officer in SOE for some time; under him was a staff including a GII, a GIII, a Staff Captain, an Intelligence Officer, Quartermaster, and various others. Mrs Hasluck was still working in the office, acting now as Albanian expert and adviser. She was delighted to see us and gave us a moving welcome. 'Well,' she asked, 'and how did you like them?' Knowing her love for Albania and all things Albanian, I gave her as rosy a picture as possible and concealed from her my feelings on the more unpleasant aspects of our time there.

We were taken first to see Brigadier Keeble, still in command of the SOE office in Cairo; he took us to see Major-General Stawell. Such was the rapid expansion of SOE that this General Officer had been sent out to take overall command of the offices in Cairo and Bari. General Stawell told us that he wanted us to write a full report on our mission, and that when we had done so we would be sent to London, where various people wanted to see us; after that, we would get some leave.

Our accommodation in Cairo should have been a very gloomy and squalid flat, into which SOE normally put their agents; but Moss very kindly invited us to join him in a big house in Zamalek which he and some others were sharing. We jumped at this opportunity, and had no cause to regret it; for the time we spent in Tara, as it was named by its occupants, was, as far as I was concerned, the happiest and most amusing of the entire war.

On arrival at Tara we found a large house in its own grounds, with plenty of Egyptian servants; at that moment it had five occupants in addition to Billy Moss. These included Paddy Leigh Fermor, in the Greek section of SOE and recently returned from Crete; Arnold Breene, working in SOE HQ; and, running the house, Countess Sophie Tarnowska, a truly glamorous Pole whose husband Andrew, then serving in the Polish forces, had been a close friend of my brother John when they were up at Oxford together. A short while later we were joined by Xan Fielding, also in SOE, who came straight to Tara from Crete, where for the past six months he had been in the White Mountains with the Cretan resistance, for which he received a well-earned DSO. To complete the entourage was Pixie, an Alsatian belonging to Billy Moss, and Koulka, a mongoose belonging to Sophie. McLean also found his old

Sudanese servant Abbas, and he too joined the staff as his personal servant.

We spent a month in Cairo writing reports, and during that time there was seldom a dull moment. We lived on a lavish scale, for there was plenty of back pay to spend, and Tara became notorious for its riotous parties, and for the eccentric behaviour of its occupants. From then on, Tara became my second home.

Chapter VIII: Operation 'Concensus II'

In the previous chapters on Albania I have avoided politics; but the report we wrote on our return to Cairo had a considerable bearing on our future. It was divided into political, military and technical sections, of which the greatest and most important part was political and written by McLean; the military section was a joint effort by both of us, and I wrote the technical section.

In writing his political report McLean had some help, for in the SOE office at this period was an officer, Captain Julian Amery, who had previously worked with Albanians as long ago as 1940. Amery had been in Belgrade after the entry of Italy into the war, and had started a resistance and intelligence movement in Albania, using Albanian exiles who had fled to Yugoslavia, and Albanians from the minority in Kosovo — the much disputed area which, though in Yugoslavia, contained over 800,000 Albanians and was a very rich and fertile region.

Among the Albanians with whom Amery had conspired were Major Abas Kupi, the Zogist leader; Mustafa Gjinishi, a leading Communist who became a member of the Central Council of the LNÇ; and the three Kryeziu brothers — Gani, Hasan, and Said. But the invasion of Yugoslavia by Germany and the fall of Belgrade had compelled the conspirators to scatter, and contact ceased. Since the arrival of 'Concensus' Mission in Albania it had been partly re-established, for Abas Kupi, Mustafa Gjinishi, and Hasan Kryeziu had all been in touch with British missions, and only Gani and Said Kryeziu were missing, said to be imprisoned by the Italians in Italy.

Julian Amery, born in 1919, and so a year younger than McLean and three years younger than myself, was the son of the distinguished politician Leo Amery; he had therefore been brought up in the aroma of politics. After Eton and Oxford, he went to Spain during the civil war, which he covered for a while as a newspaper correspondent. The Second World War had started while he was on holiday on the Dalmatian Coast. He had reported to the British Embassy in Belgrade and became Assistant Press Attaché. Shortly afterwards, he was co-opted by D Organization — an early forerunner of SOE.

Slight and dark, he could have passed as a Latin or a Slav, and he knew something of both languages. With a brilliant mind and a remarkable memory, he was quick to grasp all the essential points of a problem and discard anything irrelevant; in this way he reached a logical conclusion so quickly that it almost seemed as if he had given the matter no thought at all. Physically tough, he had inherited a love of skiing and mountaineering from his father, he was brave in action, strong in his convictions, and very loyal to his friends. Politics was his chief interest, and he had a natural aptitude for it; the war, as an extension of politics, gave him the opportunity to use his abilities in the service of his country.

With Amery's help, we finished the report in a month; we drew two main conclusions:

1. The LNÇ was the principal military force with any fighting capacity in the centre and south of Albania.

2. The Nationalists in the north (Nationalists meaning all those who were not LNÇ) did not appear keen to fight the Germans; under LNÇ pressure they were, in fact, being forced into collaboration with the Germans. Meanwhile, the civil war was absorbing the time and energy of the Communist partisans.

After these conclusions we made certain suggestions, in particular:

1. The civil war could be stopped if the partisans could be persuaded to agree to neutralize, rather than to attack, the Nationalists.

2. If Tito in Yugoslavia could be persuaded to declare that the Kosovars would be allowed to decide for themselves the future of Kosovo after the war, the northern tribes and chieftains might become less sympathetic to the Germans (in 1941 the Axis powers had incorporated Kosovo within the frontiers of Albania).

3. We should back the partisans with military aid, as the most effective military force in the country. At the same time, we should maintain contact with the Nationalists and try to stop the civil war, endeavouring also to persuade the more anti-German elements to collaborate with the LNÇ movement and fight the Germans.

At the beginning of January 1944, after a very gay month in Cairo, we flew with some regrets to London, where we spent a month. McLean stayed at Claridge's and I stayed at the Ritz, while we wrote more reports, gave lectures, and were interviewed by numerous people, including Mr Anthony Eden, the Foreign Secretary, and Lord Selborne, the Minister of Economic Warfare and the head of SOE. We twice met King Zog officially, and once met him and Queen Geraldine unofficially, when Mr and Mrs Leo Amery asked us all to luncheon.

During our interview with Mr Eden, it was clear that he had carefully studied our report. He asked us a number of questions and suggested that we might like to return to Albania. He proposed that we should go to the north of the country, where we might persuade the tribes to take up arms against the Germans, and perhaps also make contact with Abas Kupi, and try to persuade him to take action against the Germans. His parting words were that if we needed any special help from him, or had any points especially for him, we must not hesitate to send him a personal signal.

Before starting my leave, I went to Tempsford in Bedfordshire to attend a course on the Eureka/Rebecca and the 'S' phone instruments. Tempsford was the airfield from which the majority of agents set out on their missions, to be parachuted into the various occupied countries of Northern Europe and France. There was also a school for SOE agents, and I found this course most interesting.

The Eureka/Rebecca was a homing device for aircraft; an operator in the field could set up a small instrument on which aircraft could home and drop supplies with remarkable accuracy, even when they could not see anything on the ground. The 'S' phones consisted of two small wireless transmitters worked by dry batteries; each set had the same fixed frequency. The operator in the field had one set, which he wore on a belt round his waist, which also contained the batteries, while the second set was carried either in an aircraft or a ship. Speech was possible between the two sets provided there was no ground between them; consequently, in Albania the set was almost useless, because there were so many mountains that speech was only possible for the short time that the aircraft was directly overhead.

After a month in London on duty, SOE HQ in Baker Street told us that we could have a month's leave. I had hoped to spend my leave with various members of my family; but after staying only a week with my mother I was recalled suddenly to Baker Street, where McLean and I were given bad news from Albania. It was reported that Brigadier Trotsky Davies and his mission had been attacked, Trotsky himself had been wounded and captured, and his mission had scattered and were on the run. Some had joined up with other missions, and the fate of the rest was unknown. Under the severest conditions of a Balkan winter, they were suffering unspeakable hardships, and the Germans were still pressing them hard. Far from carrying out operations against the Germans, they were now fully occupied with the problem of their own survival.

McLean and I were asked to go to Cairo immediately, and from there to be prepared to return to Albania and take over the command and reorganization of the missions in the north, and carry on roughly where we had left off.

We left London, therefore, early in February 1944 and reached Cairo in two days. Next morning, we went to the office to find out the latest news from Albania. With great sorrow we heard that Arthur Nicholls was dead. He had escaped with Hare, who was luckily safe, but in the first days of their escape in the snow they had both succumbed to frostbite. Nicholls's condition worsened and gangrene set in, and then a fall from a mule damaged his shoulder. After a journey, in which Nicholls endured the most unbelievable hardships with the utmost courage, he was found by Seymour who, realizing his serious condition, contacted Ihsan Toptani who rushed him to his house. A doctor was summoned and his toes were immediately amputated, but Nicholls could not recover from the combination of gangrene with the shock of the operation and the sufferings of his journey; he died within a week. Several Albanians to whom we spoke later were filled with admiration for his gallant behaviour under such incredible suffering, and his reputation for courage stood high and will long be remembered in Albania. He was posthumously awarded the George Cross.

We also received news of Duffy; he had arrived in Italy with fifteen American nurses. An American Dakota flying over Italy had lost its way and made a forced landing in Albania, near Berat. Our missions were informed and Duffy, who luckily was in the area at the time, won the race between the many British officers in Albania to reach the scene of the crash. After wandering about in the south of the country for nearly six weeks, with many exciting and interesting incidents, which Duffy related to me with relish, they were successfully evacuated by sea to Italy, none the worse. President Roosevelt took a personal interest in their predicament; they even received a supply drop which included cosmetics and silk stockings. Williamson too had been evacuated and was now on leave in England.

It was at this stage in Cairo that the plan developed for Julian Amery to join our mission. McLean was certain that our future role in Albania would be more political than military, for he would have to argue very convincingly to persuade the Albanians that to fight the Germans was more important than to fight each other. McLean would need all the support he could get for this; I was quite useless in these matters, so what better choice than Amery? McLean and Amery had been at school together and were old friends, and from what Amery and I had seen of each other during the previous months in Cairo I saw no reason why we should not make agreeable companions, even though our background and interests differed. Confident that McLean and Amery's arguments would prevail, I was still an optimistic member of the party in the hope that once action started I could be usefully employed.

We spent three carefree weeks in Cairo, staying at Tara, before going to Italy. Rowland Winn, of the 8th Hussars, joined us there. Later he was parachuted into Albania, where he broke his leg. Paddy Leigh Fermor and Billy Moss had left for Crete, announcing to all their friends in Cairo society that they were going there to kidnap the German general in command of the garrison. Their SOE friends who knew that this was in fact their intention were a bit apprehensive of their security, but their social contacts laughed it off as a good joke — until six weeks later they reappeared in Cairo, accompanied by General Kreipe, the kidnapped German garrison commander. For this most successful operation, Leigh Fermor was awarded the DSO and Moss the MC. Moss later wrote a book on this operation called *Ill Met by Moonlight*, which became a bestseller and was made into a film.

Arriving back at Bari we found Peter Kemp, who had undergone a number of hair-raising adventures in Albania since we had last seen him. He had been chased out of Kosovo by the Germans, after his whereabouts had been betrayed to them by the Kosmet (the Communist partisans in Kosovo), and he had had a number of very narrow escapes; thanks only to the help given by the Kryeziu family and Muharrem Bajraktari, he had dodged the Germans and reached Montenegro. He had been flown from the airfield at Berane, which was held by Tito's partisans, and taken back to Italy. Now he was waiting to be dropped into Poland, but for the week in Bari he greatly enlivened our evenings.

While in Bari we also visited another recent arrival from Albania, Major Anthony Quayle. Quayle was in hospital suffering from malaria, jaundice, and dysentery at the same time, and he looked pretty ill. He had taken over the running of 'Seaview' after Field had blown himself up while fishing with gelignite, and he was able to give us news of the situation in that area. Quayle, an actor of great distinction before the war, has since made his reputation as an actor, producer, and film star. Seeing him in a film (*The Guns of Navarone*) some eighteen years later, lying on a stretcher, I thought he looked just the same as he had in the hospital bed in Bari.

Our team for Albania consisted of McLean, Amery and myself; there were supposed to be spare operators and wireless sets already in the country. Now that the war had moved to Italy, it was no longer necessary for the sorties to be flown from Derna to Albania, for it was only a half-hour's flight across the Adriatic from Brindisi in a Dakota. Most of the supply dropping to the Balkans was now done by Dakotas of the United States Air Force, based on Brindisi, which was conveniently situated not far south of Bari, where the SOE office was now established.

Our first attempt to drop back into Albania was made on the exact day on which, a year before, we had dropped into Greece. Kemp, who was still in Bari, offered to come with us in the honorary capacity of dispatcher, and because his company was always welcome we accepted his offer, though we made quite certain that he did not act as dispatcher; for Kemp was inclined to be vague, and I had visions of jumping out of the aircraft with my unattached static line dangling happily behind my unopened parachute — and we did not have reserve parachutes in those days. The plan for our drop was that it should be divided into two parts: first our stores and equipment would be dropped to a DZ situated near Seymour's HQ; but because this was not a suitable DZ for the dropping of bodies, being too small and rocky, a second drop would be made at Biza. Biza was only a few minutes flight away from the first DZ, though it would mean a good day's march for us once we arrived on the ground.

We set off, and within forty-five minutes were over the first DZ; the correct signal fires were lit, we made our runs and the containers and packages were successfully dropped. We then turned towards our own DZ, but there was no sign of any fires. We circled round and round for almost two hours; each circle brought us within range of the anti-aircraft defences of Tirana, which we knew had a liberal supply of 88 mm guns. Flak burst nearby, and my natural fear (for I had been told that Dakotas blew up very easily when hit) was not improved by Kemp who, every time a shell burst near us, violently shaking the aircraft, would say, 'Are you quite all right, old boy?' However, we forgave him, for he had come equipped with a flask of grappa, which we all appreciated. Searchlights swept over the aircraft twice, and, after being jolted by several near misses, the pilot wisely decided to make for home — to the relief of us all. Later on, after our arrival in Albania, I was told by Jenkins, who had been present with the reception committee meeting us, that the officer in charge had lost his nerve and put the fires out before our arrival, refusing to light them again. We could have jumped all the time.

Luckily we only spent two more days at Brindisi, during one of which we all went out to dinner with Count Carlo Frasso in his castle. He was the owner of some of the finest woodcock shooting in Albania, with a shooting lodge near Valona, and he was able to give us information about certain of his Albanian friends who might prove useful contacts. The atmosphere over dinner was a little strange, because we all had to use assumed names, for security reasons. Among the guests was the Duke of Spoleto, a brother of my late adversary in Abyssinia, and the Duke of Aosta; he had at one time been the uncrowned king of Croatia. He questioned us closely about our relations, whom we had to invent, much to each other's amusement, and we were very relieved when he turned the conversation to underwater fishing and women. We had an excellent meal with plenty of servants in attendance, in spite of the wartime conditions.

Two days later we were off again, without Kemp, but with a British dispatcher in an otherwise all-American crew. This time we found the fires at once, but our drop was not a great success, for the pilot flashed the lights for 'Action Stations' and 'Go' far too late, and so we were all well past the DZ when the dispatcher gave the sign to jump. McLean jumped first, followed by me and then Amery. Our exits were good, but we all fell badly in a beech forest over a mile from the DZ. McLean fell among some rocks near the plain, I was well into the forest, hitting my back hard against a tree as I swung, and Amery fell in the forest a little higher up the mountain from me.

By good luck there was deep snow on the ground, and our falls were broken. Picking myself up, I shouted to the others; Amery replied but McLean did not. Amery and I rolled up our parachutes and carried them down the mountain together until we saw a light in the distance; a quarter of an hour's walk brought us to it. It proved to be McLean's torch stuck upright in the snow — McLean had positioned himself some way off in case anyone should decide to shoot at it, for we could take no chances because we knew that German patrols had been up to Biza. We were all now reunited on the ground, and knew where we were in relation to the DZ, for these were our old haunts; but it was about two hours before we were found by the British officers sent to receive us, accompanied by Jenkins and a Zogist *çeta*. We spent the rest of the night in a hut about a mile away from our old HQ, which we had left some five months previously.

The next morning, when we were repacking our parachutes, McLean and Amery discovered to their fury that they had been given the wrong sort; theirs were made of cotton, only used for the dropping of supplies and most unreliable in their opening. I felt one-up because mine was the correct type for parachutists — made of green artificial silk or nylon — but it was a disgraceful blunder by the packers in Brindisi. Later we learnt that Tito's partisans were being used as packers, which was small comfort.

We left the plain of Biza early the next morning, walking through the snow, which in some places had formed drifts of over five feet deep. At first the snow looked grey, as indeed it was, being covered with a sort of sooty ash, which we were told had drifted across Italy and the Adriatic from Vesuvius, which had recently been erupting. It had certainly blown a long way. We had heard wolves in the night, and later we crossed some large tracks in the snow; but the Albanians in our *çeta* assured us they were those of a bear.

We reached Shëngjergj for lunch, and while we were there Fred Nosi arrived with some news. He looked displeased at finding us with a Zogist *çeta*. We were not unkind enough to tax him as to what had happened to the partisan *çeta* which had been responsible for guarding Trotsky's HQ when he was captured, though we were tempted to do so. Nosi left after a while, no doubt to pass on the news of our arrival to the LNÇ. He had a small band of partisans with him, and it was clear that relations between them and our Zogist *çeta* were strained, especially as there was a blood feud in the village between the two leading families, and one had opted for the Communists and the other for the Zogists. We waited till nightfall before leaving Shëngjergj, for we were told we must take these precautions in order to arrive at our destination in the dark. In the event the journey proved very frustrating; it became a march of eight hours, because our guide continually lost the way, and we plodded up and down mountain tracks, so that even Amery lost some of his initial enthusiasm for his new surroundings. We assured him that guides often lost the way, but this did not cheer him; however, our spirits rose when, in the early hours, we arrived at our destination, a house in the village where Seymour had his HQ. We found Hare and another officer, Ian Merrett, with him.

It was good to see Hare and Seymour again, and we exchanged news, particularly of our time in London. They told us that all the stores we had dropped had been accounted for, except for three containers, one of which they knew contained 2000 sovereigns; a neighbouring village was suspected, but Seymour told us that the local Zogist leader had the matter in hand. We heard later that he had got to work on the villagers, using methods into which we deemed it prudent not to enquire, and recovered all except thirty-seven of the sovereigns.

The house serving as Seymour's HQ was well-stocked with food and drink, for he could send couriers into Tirana to shop; he had been in this house most of the winter. Apart from his own mission, he had been sheltering some of those who had managed to escape when Trotsky's HQ was captured; their numbers had grown to such proportions that Seymour had established a rear HQ in a village some way off but higher in the mountains and more secure than his own HQ, which was near the main road from Tirana.

We had sent word of our arrival to Major Abas Kupi, and the next night he arrived with a *çeta* of a hundred men; in view of the lateness of the hour, however, we agreed to defer our meeting until the following morning. This was the first of many conversations. I had not met Abas Kupi before, though McLean had, and Amery had known him in Belgrade. With the more outstanding details of his past I was familiar — how he had become King Zog's Chief of Police in the Krujë area, his own home, and how he had led the famous defence of Durazzo against the Italians in 1939, when his courageous action had held up greatly superior Italian forces, enabling his king to make his escape. This gallant action, the only resistance of any spirit put up in Albania against the Italians, had made him a national hero; but after the Italians occupied Albania he fled to Yugoslavia, where he lived with the Kryezius. It was there he had met Amery.

When the Germans invaded Yugoslavia he returned to Albania, marching across the mountains under very tough conditions; among his companions were Lieutenant-Colonel Oakley-Hill, one of the British officers who had served under General Percy in the pre-war Albanian gendarmerie, and the three Kryeziu brothers. The expedition was a failure, and Oakley-Hill had to return to Yugoslavia, where he became a prisoner, but Kupi rallied the Zogist tribes and became acknowledged the Zogist leader. He was a member of the Central Council of the LNÇ when it was originally formed at Peza in 1942; in those days the Council included non-Communists such as Abas Kupi, Baba Faja, and Myslim Peza, in the hopes of attracting a wider circle of recruits to its forces. This move of the Communists was successful as far as Baba Faja and Myslim Peza were concerned, for once political commissars were attached to them, they became little more than fireheads. Abas Kupi refused to have a commissar attached to him and remained independent.

Abas Kupi had been one of the LNÇ delegates at Mukaj, at the time of the agreement between the LNÇ and the Balli Kombëtar, and his was one of the signatures on behalf of the LNÇ. When he saw how blatantly Enver Hoxha and the partisans broke this agreement, he broke away from the LNÇ to proclaim a separate Zogist movement; now he stood alone, for he would not align himself with the Ballists, not only because they were opposed to Zog, but because he suspected them of collaboration with the Germans. He already had a British mission attached to him, and throughout the winter he had given shelter to British officers and NCOs whenever they were in need of it.

Kupi himself was illiterate, and to reach the position that he had done with such a handicap marked him as a character out of the ordinary. Apart from his bravery, which was such that songs were sung about him, his memory was astonishing. When I first met him, he was in his forties. He had greying hair and a stocky build, and was wearing a plus-four suit, a shirt done up at the collar with no tie, and on his head the white Albanian egg-cup fez, worn more commonly by the Ghegs of the north, in contrast to the flat topped fez of the Tosks of the south. Outwardly, he carried no weapon, though a noticeable bulge in one of his pockets indicated the presence of a pistol. He spoke neither English nor French, so all conversation with him had to be through an interpreter.

Quiet and reserved by nature, he had faultless manners, and by no outward sign did he ever betray his feelings. Each time I met him I liked him more, and a bond was forged between us when he once described McLean, Amery and myself to another Albanian as 'Tre majora, dy për politikë nji për luftë' (Three majors: two for politics and one for fighting).

Our first meeting lasted four hours, during which McLean outlined the purpose of our mission, stressing that we wanted the Gheg and the Zogist forces to fight the Germans. Kupi replied at length, his main point being that if he were given arms he would fight. He then left with an invitation to Amery to come and see him in a few days' time to continue the discussion.

After he had left we decided to move from Seymour's HQ, not only because we were too many mouths for him to feed, but also because rumours had reached us that the Germans suspected our presence. We therefore left the following day for Xibër, which was two days' march away. It was a lovely spring morning; the grass was bright green, the trees were in bud, and the ground was a carpet of violets, primroses, crocuses and cyclamen. Sleeping that night at a village, we marched all next day and reached Xibër in the evening; from there we sent a message to the rest of Seymour's party, who were living a further two hours' climb up the mountain. Later that night, Captain John Hibberdine arrived from the HQ above us, bringing signals for us from Bari. Wearing the Glengarry of the Cameronians, he was a quiet young man with a wry sense of humour, who had been parachuted to Kemp in Kosovo some months earlier.

The next morning, I climbed to the HQ on the top of the mountain and found a number of British officers and NCOs, about fifteen in all. Many of them had endured a hard winter; some had been on the run from the Germans. Others were in a poor state of health both physically and mentally, and one wireless operator was actually off his head. I sensed at once that their morale was very low; they had become very defensive-minded and were keen to leave Albania. It was obvious that the sooner they were evacuated to Italy for some rest and leave, the better, both for them and for the rest of the mission, because they would be a handicap in any case, whether active or inactive.

Jenkins and Jones were two exceptions. They looked and acted as they always had; no hardships or Germans would ever worry them. Though Jenkins had suffered badly from pneumonia during the winter, he showed no ill effects from it.

The first part of the kit that we had dropped was at this HQ, and I started sorting it out, and made the unhappy discovery that the three missing containers were the ones that included all our personal stuff. This was a great blow, for it had included all the books I had chosen, our rolls of films, and my operational camera.

Back in Xibër I discussed with McLean the problem of these men I had just seen, and we sent a signal to Bari — all our signals were directed there now — with the result that soon afterwards approval was given for their evacuation.

A few days later Amery left for his visit to Kupi, and a little later Major Richard Riddle and Lieutenant Jack Taylor arrived. Riddle had come from the Dibër area to see McLean and give him a report on the situation there, and Taylor was an American OSS officer seconded from the United States Navy.

Next day a signal came announcing that Alan Hare had been awarded an immediate MC, which delighted us all. During the attack on Trotsky's HQ he had behaved with conspicuous gallantry, refusing to leave the side of his wounded brigadier until Trotsky gave him a direct order to go. In the days that followed he had suffered considerably, and frostbite had cost him a toe.

When McLean had decided about the officers and men at the mountain headquarters — most of whom were to be evacuated while others were to reinforce existing missions — he sent signals asking all the missions when he and they could meet. The missions now in north Albania were: firstly, Seymour and Hare nearby, whose main contact was Abas Kupi; Neel in the far north of the Kukës area, in touch with Gani Kryeziu; and Riddle in the Dibër area, with Muharrem Bajraktari.

In a few days' time Amery returned from his talks with Abas Kupi. In short, Kupi said he would fight the Germans if given arms, whereas our brief was to give arms to people only *after* they had done so. However, Kupi was about to go on a two-week tour of his area and had invited McLean and Amery to accompany him.

When McLean and Amery set out on their tour they left me to run the HQ, and I had plenty to do. To begin with, I had to make arrangements, both with Bari and with local guides, for the disposal of the surplus officers and NCOs. As soon as possible I sent them all off in a southerly direction; the plan was that they should pass through the partisan areas and reach 'Seaview', from where they would be picked up and taken to Italy. It was a long journey to the coast, but once they were there a submarine or motor torpedo boat could pick them up, and then it was only a two-hour run across the Adriatic to Italy. They would have to keep clear of German patrols, and the sea crossing had the additional hazard of enemy aircraft.

Once they had all gone, I had to reorganize the HQ completely. Before McLean left, he and I decided to split into an Advanced and Rear HQ, both for practical and administrative reasons; we often had visits from officers and Albanians who needed accommodation and food, and we had to receive supply drops. Our present HQ was small and inconvenient, and none too secure because so many people knew about it. I therefore had to find two new camp sites, one handy for a dropping zone, and as secure as possible but also comfortable and near such necessities as water. Supply drops were expected shortly, so I had to work fast.

Happily, I was not left alone, for I still had with me: Hare, Hibberdine, Merrett, Jones, Jenkins and Corporal Otter, the wireless operator. In addition, we had a number of Albanian and Italian camp followers.

There were three Italians, two of whom remained with us until we left Albania. Two were officers, Captain Franco and Lieutenant Mario. Franco was thickset and tough, with little of the Latin in his appearance — he was fair and wore a military moustache; a native of Florence, he proved himself a brave officer on a number of occasions. Mario, a good deal younger than Franco, was dark and good-looking; he had a fine voice, and we often persuaded him to sing for us. His home was in Naples, for which he was homesick; he became great friends with Merrett.

The third, Sergeant Pettini, had been a medical orderly and had attached himself to Hare as his bodyguard and general factotum. He was devoted to Hare, had nursed him continuously since he had contracted frostbite, and contributed greatly to his recovery. He was useful to me because he was a good organizer; he exercised a much more effective control over the other Italians than their officers. He intensely disliked all Albanians, with the exception of Abas Kupi, with whom he was friendly and for whom, he told me, he had a great admiration.

Of the Albanian camp followers, the three interpreters and my personal servant-cum-bodyguard were the four most important. They were all very different in type and character. The first was Shaqir Trimi, dark and slight; he was a schoolmaster from Shëngjergj, a Zogist in politics, who spoke good English. He usually wore a shirt, riding breeches and stockings, and a white fez. He was seldom able to hide his emotions, which ranged from gaiety and laughter when all was going well, to intense worry and a face that greyed with fear when things were going badly. He was invaluable at the base, interpreting at the conferences with Kupi, and keeping everyone amused with his jokes, but he was not a man of action.

The second interpreter was Halit Kola, brother to a Gheg chieftain called Bilal Kola, whose allegiance was to Kupi; he was a tall, fair, wiry man, who favoured the Moslem style of dress, including the baggy trousers. He spoke French, but no English, had a good voice, and owned a guitar, which accompanied him everywhere, and he often sang for us. Always cheerful and very brave, if sometimes foolhardy, he was a useful companion on reconnaissances and actions involving violence or the risk of it.

The third interpreter was Veli Hasan. He was a tall, fair, thickset Tosk whose English was only moderate, and he always dressed in battledress with a black beret, looking like a typical British soldier — an appearance which his bearing and behaviour enhanced; no doubt it stemmed from the days when he was a gendarme and orderly to General Percy, the British head of the Albanian gendarmerie before the Italian occupation. He was a serious man of rather slow reactions, who seldom smiled. He had no political feelings but was completely reliable and courageous, both in and out of battle.

My servant-bodyguard was Asslan, an elderly man who always dressed in the Moslem style, for in normal life he was a *hoj* or priest; as such he could read and write Arabic, though he spoke no English, in spite of which we got on well with signs and my improving though limited Albanian. Although I could not speak the language fluently, I had a large vocabulary, which helped considerably. He played the mandolin well, sang and danced adequately, but was a bit slow-witted. He was very loyal and reliable, and stayed with me until I left the country.

I should add that when we finally left Albania, these four men remained behind. Asslan did not want to leave, but we feared for the safety of the others and asked our Bari office if they might be evacuated with us; but our urgent request was refused. We were compelled to abandon these men who had served us so loyally, and who by so doing had compromised their position with the partisans. An officer was even sent in the boat that evacuated us with the sole purpose of ensuring that these instructions were obeyed. We all realized that the hazards of war and the remorseless pressures of international politics take no account of personal or family feelings, but our parting was one of the saddest moments of my life, and I know that McLean's and Amery's hearts were equally heavy.

Long afterwards, we heard that Halit had escaped to the mountains and joined his brother in fighting the partisans, but I never heard his ultimate fate. Shaqir and Veli were captured by the partisans, tortured, and imprisoned on charges of helping the British. They certainly had helped, and they had even saved the lives of British officers in Albania in the common struggle against the German and Italian occupiers; but their chief motive was to serve the best interests of their country, and they were far greater patriots than the men who accused them.

Chapter IX: Civil War

When McLean and Amery left with Abas Kupi they only meant to be away for a two-week tour of Mati and Krujë, but they were delayed by German activities, and it was three weeks before they reappeared. During that time, I set up a new HQ. I chose the advanced base in a beech forest near the top of Mount Bastar, about a hundred feet below the summit, which is over 3000 feet high. After a few minutes' climb to a col, one had a wonderful view across the valley which separated us from the next range of mountains. Beyond this range, foothills led down to the plain of Tirana. One day, Hare and I watched aircraft bombing Tirana and saw the flak bursting around them and heard the noise of the guns and bombs. The only drawback to this site was that it was a fifteen-minute walk to the nearest water point, a spring, so we organized a supply system of mules carrying jerricans. We had so many visitors and guests that we restricted them to our rear HQ, which we named 'The Leave and Transit Camp'.

We had several supply drops, all carried out very inaccurately; indeed, for the rest of our time in Albania the dropping by the American pilots in their Dakotas compared very unfavourably with that of the RAF pilots in the Halifaxes. The Americans usually dropped from very high altitudes, making only a very few runs with very long sticks, which resulted in our stores being scattered for miles; of the total supplies dropped to Concensus II, nearly 50 per cent were not recovered by our mission. No doubt the locals benefited, and we suspected our guards also of helping themselves. In this respect, partisan discipline was better than that of the Zogists; they seldom, if ever, stole supplies, for this offence might well result in the offender being shot. The Zogist *çetas*, on the other hand, being less soldierly, had little discipline, and few morals about purloining our equipment.

After one luncheon party, all the cutlery disappeared. We suspected our guests, but we were wrong: for the culprit turned out to be Amery's servant Kalaver, who was a real scoundrel. He and Amery were devoted to each other, and all efforts by McLean and me to make Amery sack him failed — the trouble being that he never stole from his master but always from others.

Among the visitors who came to our HQ while McLean and Amery were away was Ihsan Toptani. I knew all about him from the help he had given to Nicholls, and for his efforts to reconcile the LNÇ and the Nationalists — he was, as I have mentioned, the moving spirit behind the meeting at Mukaj. Approaching early middle age and with a receding hairline, he spoke excellent English and also German, having been educated in Vienna. He had just come from his house outside Tirana and looked too tidy and clean to be taken for a man from the mountains. In his plus-fours, he looked as though he was about to set out on a round of golf. He came from a distinguished family of Albanian patriots, and was a most useful ally for our mission, since he was not aligned with any political party, though he had views of his own; he was on good terms with most of the political leaders, whether they were Communists, Zogists, Ballists, or members of the German sponsored government, and he had contacts with the Germans too. He stayed with us all day and said he would come again when McLean and Amery returned.

The American, Jack Taylor, who was a very useful member of our HQ, left for Burrel one day to receive a new wireless operator, who was being dropped: our DZ on Mount Bastar was too narrow for anything but supply drops. He came back fuming at the inaccuracy of his fellow countryman's dropping, and immediately sent them a rude signal. The operator had landed a long way from the DZ, though fortunately he was unhurt. This very welcome reinforcement was Sergeant Collins, a regular Gunner by profession and a Newcastle Geordie by upbringing. He was to share a great part of my life later on in the Far East. For the moment, I knew him only as a wireless operator and a specialist trained in Dakota and Lysander receptions — the RAF would never land and pick up anyone by Lysander unless someone on the ground had been on one of their pick-up courses. He was the only man in Albania with this training, and we hoped to get a Lysander service going.

At last McLean and Amery came back. They had made some progress with Kupi, who had agreed to fight without further arms supplies, providing he received a letter from King Zog ordering him to do so — he even said he would fight with his bare hands if so ordered by his King. When in London we had actually asked King Zog to write a letter to Kupi, and he had done so, but the Foreign Office had refused to let us take it. I did not know the reason but presumed they did not wish it to be implied that His Majesty's Government recognized King Zog. They were sensitive to being accused of this by the Americans, who were already critical of the support we had given to the King of Greece. It is worth recalling that the Americans had a deep distrust of our support for any form of monarchy, to the extent that when civil war raged in Athens, the American Embassy ran up a white flag and declared themselves neutral in the struggle between the Government and the Communists. The British immediately sent help in the form of troops, and both Americans and Greeks might well remember that this was the main reason why Greece is not Communist today.

We considered it so important to get this letter from King Zog that, for the first time, McLean availed himself of Mr Eden's offer to communicate direct; on 23 May he sent a signal which I quote:

> For Eden. Kupi leader Albanian Zogist party has agreed collaborate with us and fight Germans. He realises there can be no question of recognizing Zog but asks that the king send him personal telegram followed by letter confirming his decision. Consider there is grave danger that without this message of encouragement Kupi may go the way of Mihailovic[14] and for this reason have availed myself of your offer to send you personal telegram in emergency.

A few days later McLean and Amery left for another tour, this time for the Dibër area, where they were to meet Riddle. They took Hibberdine with them, who was being sent further north to join Neel. I missed both his company and his work at the base, for he had been extremely useful, but Taylor took his place and proved himself remarkably versatile; he could turn his hand to most things, and on one occasion had even successfully amputated the fingers of a boy who had let a grenade explode in his hand.

---

[14] General Mihailovic was the leader of the right-wing Cetnic forces, loyal to the king, who fought against the Germans when they invaded Yugoslavia. Later, when Tito's forces turned against him, Mihailovic was drawn into collaboration with the Germans, though he continued to help Allied officers. After the war, he was tried by the Tito government and executed.

After McLean's departure, Hare left for Tirana with Pettini; it was known there were potential deserters in the area, and Hare's job was to spread rumours, or 'black propaganda', to encourage desertion.

The same day, Halit Kola arrived with rumours that some Americans had bailed out in the plain below. This was confirmed the next day, when an American sergeant was brought in by the Zogists after bailing out near Tirana. The following day, four more American aircrew arrived. They were from a bomber that had crashed after being badly hit by flak during a raid on Vienna. 'Where are we?' was one of the first questions they asked. 'In Albania,' they were told. 'Gee, I thought we were in Yugoslavia,' replied one. I sent them to the Leave and Transit camp. After a short stay there, we organized guides and an escort, and they were evacuated.

Orders now came from Bari authorizing further evacuations, and Seymour, Taylor, and Lis departed. I was especially sorry to lose the help of Taylor. They all went to Berane, a landing ground in Montenegro held by Tito's partisans. They were escorted by Nik Sokoli, one of Kupi's Gheg chieftains, and a very amusing little Catholic priest, Pater Lek Luli, a staunch Zogist who always carried his tommy gun slung over his cassock. After parting from Seymour, Pater Lek Luli was handed over by the Yugoslav partisans to Mehmet Hoxha, the commissar of the Kosmet partisans.[15] This notoriously brutal man tried to extract from him the details of Abas Kupi's

---

[15] There is no doubt that the three Communist parties in Greece, Yugoslavia and Albania had a close liaison, though they were unable to give material help to each other as all were in short supply. All supplies came from the British, and at no time did the Russians send supplies to, or have a representative with, the Albanian partisans. A representative of Tito's, a sinister figure called Ali Duchanovic, was frequently seen by us with members of the *Shtab*.

negotiations with our mission; but the brave little priest refused to divulge any details, even under torture — he was flogged, had his fingers broken, and was branded with hot irons. In the end, Hoxha ordered his throat to be cut. They also murdered Seymour's old servant Rifat, after inflicting the same tortures on him; he knew nothing of the talks and therefore was in no position to divulge anything, for Rifat was a harmless old peasant whose only crime had been to serve Seymour loyally since he had dropped to us at Shtyllë.

On 5 June I was woken up early by our Italian mess waiters, Mario and Elezo, who rushed into my hut shouting, '*Invasione! Invasione!*' I seized my pistol and leapt up in alarm, but it turned out that they had been listening to the wireless. When I listened to the next BBC news broadcast, it confirmed that the Second Front had started in Normandy. We were all thrilled. The end of the war was a stage nearer. That night we had a big celebration.

Two days later I received sad news from Bari: Philip Leake had been killed. He had dropped into Albania mainly because he thought it his duty, as the staff officer responsible for sending officers into the field, to see for himself the conditions under which they worked. He was with a mission encamped near Përmet which was strafed by German fighters, and an unlucky bullet or bomb splinter had hit him in the head and killed him instantly. It was a bad blow to our mission, for not only did we know and like him personally, but we had confidence in his judgement, which we lacked in the other members of his staff; later events were to prove how serious was his loss.

His death was shortly followed by more bad news — the Foreign Secretary's reply to McLean's personal signal. It stated that he sympathized with us but regretted he could not commit himself to obtaining the letter from King Zog. It ended by urging us to 'keep the pot boiling'. Two days later McLean and Amery arrived, to my great relief, because Abas Kupi and his *çeta* had been waiting for them in our camp for the past two days and had eaten us right out of food. Luckily we had a supply drop while they were there, which was well-timed not only because of the extra food, but we hoped it would impress them with the chance of arms being dropped as easily as food.

The day after their return, McLean and Amery spent the morning discussing what they would say to Kupi, and most of the afternoon and evening talking to him. I did not envy them, firstly because they had no letter or signal from King Zog to show, and secondly because Kupi had returned to his earlier stance that he would not fight until he had first received arms. I was getting pretty fed up at the thought of further inactivity. I can't have been much good at hiding my feelings, for I overheard McLean remark to Amery, 'David seems to be getting restless again; we must find him something to blow up.'

Shortly after this, Kupi delighted me by saying he would show his good faith by helping us blow up a bridge and he would fight if necessary. This excellent news raised my morale, rapidly flagging at the political trend of our mission, because at last I would have something worthwhile to do. Kupi and his *çeta* left, planning to meet me in two days' time.

I decided to take Jenkins and Veli with me on this operation; we spent the next day packing up a large stock of explosives, and that night we left to rendezvous with Kupi. Our mules also carried two thousand sovereigns destined for him.

On meeting Kupi we quickly got down to the work of planning the operation, and after poring over maps and using Kupi's local knowledge, we decided that the Gjole bridge would be our target. It carried the main Tirana-Durazzo road over the Tiranë River, was the third largest bridge in Albania, and was in frequent use by German convoys, so it was a worthy target. Kupi then said he would place a *çeta* of twelve picked men under my command for the operation, and their leader would be Ramiz, normally his personal bodyguard. Ramiz was a small, dark young man, with a merry twinkle in his eye, full of fun, who proved to be quite fearless on operations and an excellent ally.

The first move was to get the explosives to within a reasonable distance of the bridge, and then to carry out a reconnaissance of the bridge itself. Saying farewell to Kupi, we moved off. Our *çeta* with the column of mules climbed into the Krujë mountains and, after a day's march, descended to the plains.

We reached a village that night, where I fell asleep at once. The next day I changed into civilian clothes, left the party behind and, accompanied only by Ramiz and another member of his *çeta* called Bardhok, walked for two hours to one of Kupi's farms, where we had an excellent lunch. After lunch we reached the main road. It seemed very strange to me to be walking along it with convoys of German lorries driving past within a few feet of us, paying no attention.

At last we came to Ura e Gjolës (Gjolë Bridge); it was larger than I had expected. When all was clear, I took measurements of the road and photographs for my records, and then went underneath to inspect the piers. Luckily at this time of year the river was fairly low, and the two largest piers were on dry land; to my delight I found that not only were demolition chambers already incorporated in the concrete piers, but that, in their thoroughness the Germans had marked against them the number of kilos of explosive required for the job. This was a good check on my calculations, with which they agreed; but I realized at once that I had not brought enough explosives, so we went back to the farm and I sent Bardhok off in haste with a note to our HQ asking for more.

They took three days to arrive. While the main party stayed in a village in the foothills, I stayed with Ramiz at Kupi's farm, going each day to the road to take down details of German transport and identifications of their troops. We had one bit of bother at the farm, when a man arrived who claimed to be the leader of a Zogist *çeta*, saying that the Germans knew we were there and that we should leave at once. Ramiz and I both agreed that he was unnecessarily scared; so, thanking him for his advice, we took no action.

That night we heard a good deal of shooting near the road and saw Verey lights going up. This puzzled us and made us think the man might have been right. In the morning, Ramiz said he would go and investigate; he returned shortly to say that it had only been a local blood feud, in which four people had been killed, but the Germans on the road had been alarmed at the shooting and had fired the Verey lights. 'Windy,' I thought to myself.

On 20 June the mules arrived with the extra explosives, and the main party joined us the same night at Kupi's farm. Jenkins and I spent all next day in preparing the gelignite; it had to be taken out of wooden boxes and the sticks moulded together and repacked, which not only gave us both a splitting headache but made me sick as well. It is a known fact that handling gelignite in some way poisons one through the pores, with these unpleasant results.

We left at eleven that night, taking the mules to a position out of sight of the road, about a hundred yards away, where we unloaded the explosives. Then we sent the mules back to the village in the hills. The men from the *çeta* ferried the explosives under the bridge, while I did my best to curb my impatience, for on occasions like this speed and silence are vital. They were sadly lacking. My shouted whispers had to be contained for half an hour while a German staff car was tiresome enough to have a puncture on the bridge and the occupants changed a wheel; some of us were actually under it at the time, not daring to move back for more explosives, for fear of being seen. One German reminded us of his presence by urinating over the side, but luckily he did not score a direct hit on any of us.

After the German staff car had moved off, the rest of the explosives were dumped under the bridge. We sent all our helpers away, Ramiz telling them to keep within calling distance in case anything went wrong and we needed help. Ramiz, Veli, Jenkins and I remained to carry out the final preparations; we were all very tense and excited, and worked feverishly — Jenkins and I doing the detailed technical work, while Veli and Ramiz kept a lookout for any possible intruders, in case anyone walking on the bridge heard us. Packing the explosives in position, linking the charges, and placing the detonators and guncotton boosters, took over two hours. During this time several German vehicles crossed the bridge, for the Germans favoured movement by night owing to the daylight RAF attacks on their transport. Every time a lorry crossed overhead our voices dropped to a whisper, though even if we had been singing the Germans in the vehicles would never have heard us.

In technical jargon, there were three demolition chambers on each pier, into each of which we put a mixture containing 100 lb of gelignite, plastic, and ammonal; then we added four beehive charges to the top of the pier, between it and the span, where there was a gap. The junction box had four leads from it, and the whole system was initiated by two time pencils, in case one of them failed. The time pencils had a ten-minute delay.

Finally, the bridge was ready for blowing and I inserted and squeezed the time pencils; preferably we should have used safety fuse, a much simpler and more reliable method of initiating a charge, but we had none in Albania at that time. Then we went on to the road and scattered a few tyre bursters (small explosive charges disguised to resemble mule droppings, which would blow a large hole in the tyre of any vehicle that ran over one) and made off to a position about two hundred yards away to watch. Within five minutes, two vehicles had run over the tyre bursters and stopped on the bridge.

I looked at my watch closely when the ten minutes were up, and then at the bridge. Nothing happened. After a further ten minutes, I turned to Jenkins and said, 'Something has gone wrong, and I'm going back to see what it is.' 'Be careful, sir,' he replied with his usual grin as I started off. Because of the Germans on the bridge, my progress was very slow for I had to crouch down, dodge from cover to cover behind rocks and bushes, and at times crawl. When I had covered about half the distance the ground shook and, with a flash and a tremendous explosion, the bridge went up, complete with the Germans on it. Concrete debris began to fall all round me, but luckily I was not hit. I quickly rejoined the others and we moved off happily to where the rest of the *çeta* were waiting. They were delighted with the result and kept saying to me 'Shum mire' ('very good'). Since we expected German reactions, we did not waste time on the plains, but, after collecting the mules, returned over the mountains to our base. When we got there the *çeta* eagerly recounted our success to all their friends, but by then I was feeling awful from a recurrence of malaria and retired to bed.

Kupi arrived the next morning to announce that the bridge had been completely destroyed, two spans having fallen into the river; he added that a member of the Toptani family who lived nearby had had all his windows shattered by the blast. An orgy of mutual backslapping followed; not only had the operation been a success, but Kupi had at last proved his willingness to fight.

A few days later we sent most of our rear HQ to Matsukull, a village where we could more easily and safely receive the supplies that we now expected to be dropped for Kupi. Kupi had already given us a list of his arms requirements; now that he had started fighting, we assumed that his supplies would follow, as signals from the Bari office had promised.

McLean, Hare, and Amery left a few days later to stay with Ihsan Toptani at his house near Tirana, to meet various political leaders from the town. They were away for five days, but before leaving they had arranged with Kupi to call a meeting of all the Nationalists and the Gheg chieftains from the north; it was to be held in two weeks' time, and we hoped to co-ordinate plans there for action against the Germans.

The day after McLean and Amery returned from their visit to Tirana was the blackest in the history of our mission. Hare, who had left them to go to visit Kupi, returned with the worst possible news: the 1st Partisan Brigade of the LNÇ had attacked the Zogist forces at Shëngjergj, had driven them out, and were advancing in our direction; Kupi was threatening to move forward with his troops and engage the partisans.

The civil war had now reached us. All our high hopes of getting Kupi to fight the Germans had been shattered, for he would obviously have to move to protect his own region and its villages from the ravages of the partisans. That night Kupi arrived at our camp, accompanied by Said Kryeziu, Dan

Kaloshi, and some of his *çeta* leaders. The main topic of conversation was how to stop the civil war; we sent urgent signals to Bari asking the BLOs with the partisans to do all they could to restrain them, and Kupi sent a signal to King Zog asking for orders. We also decided to send Hare to Shëngjergj to negotiate with the LNÇ leaders.

Meanwhile the conference had not been cancelled, so we all moved north, descending into the Mati valley, accompanied by Kupi's *çeta*; after a welcome bathe in the Mati we moved on past the burnt out town of Burrel and, after a further day's march, reached our rear HQ at Matsukull. Here we stayed the night, while more of Kupi's chieftains and their *çetas* arrived, among them Muharrem Bajraktari. Next day we moved to the agreed rendezvous, the glade of Zogolli, a strip of boulder-strewn grassland that ran for a long distance through the middle of a forest.

That night he had had news of fresh attacks by the partisans on Kupi's men, and only with difficulty did we persuade them to hold the conference the next day. We all sat in a circle at the edge of the glade, and as if the news was not depressing enough, a thunderstorm made it worse, the proceedings being enlivened only by the appearance of a lunatic, an unkempt figure who screamed and gesticulated at us. Amery asked Muharrem Bajraktari what this poor creature was shouting, to which he replied, 'He wants us to fight the Germans, but of course he's mad!' 'I wish he'd bite a few of the people here,' I said in an aside to my British colleagues. The talks now took on a different turn, the main point of discussion being not how to fight the Germans, but how to keep the civil war in check.

A signal from Bari arrived during the conference to say that Captain Victor Smith would be dropped that night, with proposals for halting the civil war; so his appearance was anxiously awaited. He dropped safely, together with a wireless operator (who I thought was drunk) and told us of the proposals. Kupi and the LNÇ should both be invited to send delegates to Bari. Kupi agreed at once, saying that he would like to go himself and take Said Kryeziu with him.

The conference then broke up; everyone dispersed in different directions, while our own mission, with Smith and Said Kryeziu, set off for our advanced HQ at Bastar, where we hoped Hare would be awaiting us.

We marched for two days, passing through all the signs of preparation for civil war; Zogist *çetas* were taking up positions, and in the distance smoke could be seen rising from Zogist villages which the partisans were burning down. We deemed it prudent to send on a messenger ahead to warn Hare of our arrival, but he returned with appalling news: the partisans had overrun our HQ at Bastar, and captured Hare, Corporal Otter, the wireless sets and all our supplies.

To make matters worse, Smith now informed us that the office in Bari had, behind our backs, made the invidious arrangement with the LNÇ leaders that any BLOs 'found' with the National or Zogist forces would be 'escorted' to the coast for evacuation. We knew that this meant being treated as prisoners, if not shot on the spot. As our first thought was to keep contact with Kupi, we decided to turn back; at all costs we had to avoid falling into the hands of the partisans.

Smith, however, having completed half his mission with Kupi, now had to carry out the other half with the partisans. He was a fresh-faced young man with a large jutting jaw. He was wearing shorts, and this dress, coupled with such enthusiastic remarks as 'we could stop the civil war by getting the leaders to Bari and knocking their heads together', led us to christen him behind his back 'the Boy Scout'. Having said goodbye, the Boy Scout set off to join the partisans and put Bari's proposals to their leaders. When he finally caught up with Enver Hoxha, the proposals were rejected out of hand.

We were now in something of a fix. Our HQ had gone, and matters became even worse when reports reached us that the partisans were sending out determined patrols to capture us at all costs, thus cutting off Kupi from any further contacts with the British.

We were already out of touch with him; and now we heard that the Germans were in Burrel, which cut us off from our rear HQ at Matsukull. Our party now consisted of McLean, Amery, Said Kryeziu, Corporal Davis the wireless operator and his set, interpreters, mulemen, personal servants and me.

We spent the next few days in a large beech forest, which was cold and wet — for it rained a great deal — hiding from partisans and Germans alike. We were near a stream, but though the mules happily ate beech leaves off the branches, we all were running short of food. We sent some of the retainers out to reconnoitre; they returned with rumours of partisans everywhere. Clearly they were becoming very scared, some of them asking if they could return to their homes: obviously they did not want the partisans to find them working with us.

We could not stay in the forest indefinitely, so we made a plan to split up; Amery and Kryeziu would try to break through to Kupi, McLean and Davis would stay where they were, keeping contact with Bari, and I would try to reach our rear HQ at Matsukull. We decided that I should leave first, but Shaqir would not come with me; his face was greyer than ever with fear, so I set off with only a guide and Asslan, my bodyguard cum servant.

We spent two days in the forests, but as the tracks were patrolled by the partisans we avoided them, and the going through the woods was very hard. The only food I had in the first thirty-six hours was a piece of stale maize bread out of Asslan's pocket, and when we did finally emerge from the forest and descend into the Mati valley, the frightened villagers refused us shelter. Eventually the guide lost his nerve and refused to go on, so I decided to return to McLean. We found him in the same place, and Amery still with him.

We planned to join forces: Amery, Said Kryeziu and I, together with our mules, would try to cross the Krujë-Burrel road where it ran between the partisan and the German lines. We succeeded in doing this during the night, although at times we were so close to our pursuers we could hear their voices. Then we split up, Amery and Said making for Kupi's HQ while I set off for Matsukull. That evening I reached a village, passing on the way a very pretty girl — this was worthy of note, as I saw so few in Albania. My guide took me to the house of a Zogist, who was very friendly and hospitable. Just as I had gone to sleep on that first night, he rushed in crying that the partisans were in the village; leading me out of the back of the house, he made me hide in a drain until they had passed — they were only a patrol.

Rumours arrived frequently, and we could hear firing and the crump of mortars in the distance; from what I was told I gathered that Germans, Balli Kombëtar, gendarmes, Zogists and partisans were having a free for all. Several rumours concerning our rear HQ at Matsukull came in, some alleging that it had been captured by the Germans, and others by partisans.

My military training coming to the fore, I thought that this called for an appreciation of the situation; I reproduce it as I wrote it in my diary at the time. My spirits could not have been too bad, or I should not have been so facetious:

> I cannot go North — Huns; South — Partisans; East — a violent battle; West — robber bands. Conclusion — I am bitched. Plan — to stay in this house. Reasons — it is very comfortable, food is plentiful, I get a bottle of excellent raki before each meal, and a good *meze* of meat, cucumber, garlic, onions and cheese.

Two days later my host suddenly rushed into the room and announced that about fifty partisans were only five minutes away, and that I must go. I hurriedly packed my very few possessions into my pockets, strapped on my pistol, and went outside, where I found an escort of gendarmes awaiting me. My host assured me that this was in order, though I was somewhat puzzled because I thought the gendarmes were supposed to be working with the Germans. We set off at a high speed and later on linked up with a Zogist *çeta* some two hundred strong; after a march of several hours, we reached a village where I found McLean and Amery.

From them I learnt that the Zogist counterattack was going well and that the partisans were withdrawing on all fronts. Later in the day we moved to Bastar and joined Kupi, who had another two hundred men with him. We agreed with him that I should go and reconnoitre the coast, and once again he kindly lent me Ramiz and Bardhok. I got on very well with them both, in spite of the fact that neither of them spoke a word of English, which was very good for my Albanian.

Next day, leaving McLean and Amery at Bastar, I moved off with my two companions, and that night reached the house of a Zogist leader, Xhemal Herri, where we slept. Xhemal Herri, who had been Chief of King Zog's Secret Police, had at the moment a *çeta* of over two hundred men, including Italians, six escaped Russian prisoners-of-war, and a German deserter. We moved on early next morning to Ihsan Toptani's house at

Topize, where we had breakfast with Colonel Jahja Çaçi (known to the British as 'Hiya Charlie'), and then went on to a farm of Kupi's, where we met Ibrahim Farka, whom Kupi had told to help us reach the coast.

After luncheon we took a car, passing a German convoy on the road. Eventually we reached a Bektashi monastery, whose incumbent monk was a Zogist. After a first-rate dinner with our host, we climbed into the car again and drove on down the road. By this time, it was dark. I had a fright when a German soldier appeared in the road and signalled the car to stop, for I was in uniform and heartily wished I could have made myself smaller. However, he was only slowing us down because there had been a traffic accident, and he waved us on without looking inside. Eventually Ramiz, Bardhok, and I got out of the car; Ibrahim Farka, informing us that it was only two hours walk to the coast, drove away.

Then a strange thing happened; as we were walking along the road, very quietly and suddenly a German soldier appeared behind us on a bicycle, and, as he drew level with us, he dismounted and started to walk with us. We all strolled along together while he made polite conversation in broken Albanian and Italian, keeping it up for twenty minutes. His Albanian was worse than mine, but I managed to ask him his unit, where it was, and where was the nearest German post, all of which he kindly told us. He offered me a packet of cigarettes, to which I replied, 'Nuk pië' ('I do not smoke') in my best Albanian; after a while, he jumped on his bicycle and rode off. My companions thought this a huge joke and Ramiz kept slapping his sides with laughter, for I was wearing British battledress, a major's crowns, a parachute badge and medal ribbons on my breast; my only civilian clothing was the white Albanian fez I always wore; yet there I had been, happily walking along talking to a German soldier. I often wonder who that German thought I was; perhaps he knew and did the only possible thing, for we were all armed and could easily have murdered him; in fact I considered doing so, but at that moment did not want to attract attention to our movements.

Soon after this, we branched off the main road and took a smaller one until we came to a village not far from the sea, where Ramiz had a fisherman friend. He knocked quietly on the door, for it was past midnight and we did not want all the dogs in the village to start barking; after a whispered conversation with the man who opened it, we were let in. When Ramiz explained the purpose of our visit, his friend told him the coast was heavily guarded by Germans and said where some of their posts were. I said that I would like to go and verify some of these for myself the next day, but the snag was that I was still in battledress. As usual, Ramiz had an answer; next morning he left us, shortly to reappear carrying a gendarme's uniform which he said he had borrowed from a friend. He said he was about my size, and so I changed into it and found it an adequate fit; moreover, the stripes proclaimed me as a sergeant.

I spent five days in this uniform, checking a number of German positions in the Cape Rodoni area and marking them on my map. It was clearly strongly held, for both the north and south shores of the cape had numerous posts, barbed wire defences, and several minefields. For evacuation purposes it was out of the question, and so I decided to try the coast further north, whereupon Ramiz said it would be easier to travel by car and he would fix it. He did, but not quite in the way I intended.

The next day a gendarme sergeant appeared at the house; this was the friend of Ramiz who owned the uniform I was wearing; we all set off together, with me feeling a little self-conscious. At the end of the village we stopped at a track junction, which Ramiz indicated led to Germans, or 'Tedeschi' as he called them; his information was confirmed in a few minutes when a German lorry drove down towards us, and which to my horror our gendarme friend flagged to a halt. After a few words with the driver, whom apparently he knew, we all piled into the back, where we found some German soldiers. I thought this a bit much, for what my limited Albanian had led me to expect from Ramiz was a lift in a car, not a lorry full of German soldiers. However, we drove on, joining the main road and turning northwards. We had not been going for long when the lorry drew to a halt with a shriek of brakes. Everyone leapt out and I joined them, for the reason was all too clear.

RAF Beaufighters now made a habit of patrolling this road by day, shooting up everything in sight — not only German transport but civilian vehicles, ox carts, mules, and on one occasion our courier; now it was me. We lay in the ditch as the fighters zoomed overhead, but luckily for us the shower of bullets hit the road some way off, for the pilot had overshot his target. The German in the ditch beside me shook his fist at the disappearing aircraft, and, to show there was no ill-feeling, I did the same. When the fighter failed to return, we climbed aboard again and continued for a few miles, until the gendarme beat on the roof of the driver's cabin. It stopped, we got off, and the lorry drove away.

The strip of coast we saw next was unguarded and it had distinct possibilities; after I had noted down the details of the beach we retraced our tracks, and in due course I found McLean at Valias, in another house of Ihsan Toptani's. A stay there was always a wonderful treat, for his house was completely civilized and modern, and my great joy was to lie soaking in a hot bath; I even took pleasure in pulling the plug of the lavatory, for that was something out of the ordinary for us, who were accustomed to a box-like cabin protruding over an outer wall with a hole in the floor.

Chapter X: On the run and evacuation

We left Ihsan Toptani's house the following morning, and after some hours' walk came to a village where we found Amery, Said Kryeziu, and Davis in a very squalid house. This became our HQ for a week, at the end of which we were all glad to leave, for it was dirty, smelly and flea-ridden, and food was scarce until our courier eventually arrived. We were all miserably ill in turn — McLean and Amery had tummy troubles and I had malaria again and ran a high temperature for several days. It was a relief when we left this hovel for more congenial surroundings and moved up into the foothills, from where we had a good view of Tirana. Our new HQ was very pleasant, situated in an olive grove where there was plenty of cover both from the sun and from enemy aircraft. Better still, the security was good, with lines of escape in several directions, for with both Germans and partisans hunting us we were more conscious of our security than ever.

Signals between ourselves and Bari now flew thick and fast. Poor Davis was overwhelmed by their number, and by the length of those composed by McLean and Amery in a style calculated to impress the Foreign Office ('at the conclusion of conversations' for 'when talks ended'). The use of diplomatic language and confusing words caused Bari to ask for numbers of repeats on expressions such as *ipso facto* and *sine qua non*; I therefore spent most of my time helping him with the cipher work. Davis was a particularly nice young lad from Hampshire — he looked so young that after Kupi referred to him as '*çuni*' (the youth), the nickname stuck, and thereafter he was called '*çuni*' by all. He was slight of build and did not look strong, but he had in fact excellent stamina, as well as a quick and bright intelligence. His methods were haphazard and extremely unorthodox, but nevertheless they produced the right results, for he rarely failed to make contact with Bari; he was a hard worker, and in our many crises and emergencies showed courage and coolness, his first thought always for the safety of his wireless set.

I carried out another reconnaissance from this HQ. I took Halit as well as Ramiz and Bardhok to ensure that this time there would be no language misunderstandings. The reconnaissance was uneventful except for an incident that took place at Ura e Gjolës. I wanted to photograph the bridge we had blown, for I had heard that the Germans, after six weeks' work, had built a temporary wooden one in its place. At a range of about fifty yards I was aiming my camera, standing on the bank of the river, and had taken three good shots when I heard someone shouting from the bridge in German. As I took one more photograph, bullets started to whistle past us, and so we quickly made ourselves scarce and returned to our HQ. Halit told me that while I was taking photographs there had been two sentries at the ends of the bridge, for the Germans had now put a guard on it, but I had not seen them. Sure enough, when the films were developed, one of them clearly showed a German soldier at one end of the bridge, with his rifle to his shoulder, aiming at the camera. It was very careless of me, but I must have been concentrating so hard on looking through the viewfinder that I forgot to look elsewhere.

We stayed two weeks in our camp in the olive grove. I grew very depressed at this stage, for as far as I could see our work in Albania was over, our mission had failed, and I felt that the sooner we returned to Italy the better. Long signals still flowed between McLean and Bari, for he and Amery still had some, though diminishing, hopes that a solution on the lines of the Smith proposals might yet be found, especially since Bari had told us that no supplies would be dropped to the partisans while they attacked Kupi.

However, the BLOs attached to the partisans, repeatedly told by them that Kupi was collaborating with the Germans, had absorbed these lies and signalled them to Bari. We well knew that at no time did Kupi collaborate with the Germans, but the office in Bari did not accept our assurances and consequently started once more dropping supplies to the partisans. They did so while the partisans were actually fighting Kupi and without informing us, which was a flagrant breach of their side of the agreed policy. By their deceit they completely undermined our position and cast a slur on our good faith; for when Kupi had reproached us and accused the British of supplying the partisans we had in all honesty denied it — indeed we could not believe it possible.

My depression was not improved by another bout of malaria. One night when I was feeling particularly ill I heard shooting not far off, and we suspected that either Germans or partisans were attacking Xhemal Herri's house. As the shooting came nearer we saddled up the mules; but only seventeen were there because the rest had been sent to nearby grazing, and so a good deal of petrol, the charging engine, and other supplies had to be left behind.

We moved about an hour's distance away from the base, leaving one of our bodyguards behind to see what happened. After some time, he rejoined us and told us that the partisans had first burnt down Xhemal Herri's house and were now looting our camp; he had seen them smash the charging engine. He added that, having seen a patrol move off in our direction, he had come as quickly as possible to warn us; so we moved on again, descending the mountain until we reached a wood on the edge of the plains. This proved to be the partisans' second offensive against Kupi's area, and this time they were successful, entirely thanks to the help that they had received from the British. This help took the form of arms and ammunition, mines and explosives, clothing and food, money (sovereigns), communications equipment, as well as the help and advice given by the British Liaison Officers and NCOs. They also received favourable publicity on the BBC. Without this help, bearing in mind they received none whatever from the Russians, they would not have overcome the Ballists and Zogists in the civil war. Had British aid gone the other way, Albania would have become a pro-western democracy.

We were on the run again, this time only from the partisans; we stayed in the woods for three days, in low spirits, though the four Russians who had attached themselves to us from Xhemal Herri's *çeta* proved to be amusing companions, and their singing helped to relieve our gloom. On the third day Kupi turned up, depressed by his defeat, and we had no news to cheer him. He left later to see Xhemal Herri.

The next morning the news reached us that Herri and Kupi had quarrelled violently and, after an exchange of insults, Herri had reached for his gun; but Kupi had been quicker on the draw and had fired first. Hearing the shot, Ramiz had rushed into the room, where he found Herri bleeding on the floor with a bullet wound in his head; Ramiz had finished him off with a shot from his rifle.

At the end of three days we moved back to Mukaj. After some days there we received a very disturbing signal from Bari, which read as follows:

> Following message dated August 25 received from Lyon who is with Hoxha: Met Hoxha tonight. Stated McLean,

Smiley and Seymour working against partisans with collaborators. Gave ultimatum they must be out of Albania or hand themselves over to partisans for evacuation Italy within five days of tonight. Otherwise partisan patrols will be sent out to capture them and bring them back for trial by partisan military court.

A subsequent message stated: 'Hoxha no longer considers officers with Kupi and other traitors as allied, due to their behaviour, but considers them agents of foreign reactionaries who are organizing the fight against the partisans.'

This caused some reaction in Bari, where we still apparently had friends, for an ultimatum was sent to Hoxha stating that unless he withdrew this threat immediately, all supplies to him would cease and all BLOs would be withdrawn. This ultimatum had the desired effect, and the threat was withdrawn; but it was over a week before we knew of it, and in the meantime we had received news that we had been tried by a People's Court and condemned to death *in absentia* as 'enemies of the people'.

We were pleased that Bari had shown some confidence in us, because the signals from the BLOs attached to the partisans repeated more accusations of Kupi's collaboration with the Germans, with insinuations that we knew of it and were concealing the fact. This did not speak very highly for the mentality of the BLOs concerned; to accuse brother-officers of treason, solely on the words of Albanian Communists, showed a remarkable lack of judgement. However, we understood Hoxha and his methods probably far better than the BLOs who were then with him, and even if he had withdrawn his threat, we had little confidence that he had cancelled the orders to his partisans for our capture. What action could Bari take on receiving a message from a BLO with Hoxha stating that

McLean and Smiley had been 'shot while resisting arrest', or 'shot trying to escape'?

In our determination to avoid capture by the partisans we kept to the plains, for the partisans operated mainly in the mountains and seldom ventured onto the plains in strength. Furthermore, we had received indications that the German withdrawal would not be long delayed and heard that a number of Turkoman troops with the Germans were showing signs of restlessness. Ihsan Toptani had also just arrived to tell us that the Germans had withdrawn all their 88 mm antiaircraft guns from around Tirana; more important still, he said there were rumours that the German-sponsored government was willing to take to the mountains, together with all the gendarmerie and the Albanian army, and join us. We were naturally careful not to have anything to do with the Germans, and duly signalled all this information back to Bari for instructions. While we were waiting for a reply to this signal, Kupi suddenly appeared and announced that he intended to attack the German garrison at Durazzo. This was a welcome bit of news, and we decided that I should go off to reconnoitre Durazzo with a view to recommending the best way to attack the town.

On 28 August McLean, Amery and I left Mukaj and walked to Ihsan Toptani's house; from there Toptani took us in his car to Kupi's house at Luz, where we lay down to sleep. At two in the morning I was awakened by Kupi himself, who brought me some civilian clothes — a very shabby and ill-fitting blue suit. I put this on and, still wearing my white fez, I went into the room next door, where I found Halit Kola and two gendarmerie officers. Kupi introduced them to me as Major Hamza Drini, the commander of the entire Durazzo area, and Captain Rifaat Tershana, commanding the gendarmes in Durazzo — both ardent Zogists. We drank coffee and then set off together in a truck; after about ten minutes we suddenly drew up at a barrier across the road. My heart sank, for it was guarded by German soldiers who now approached the truck, rifles at the ready, and demanded to see our documents. But my fears were groundless, for the presence of two senior gendarmerie officers in the front was sufficient for the Germans to signal us through without checking the credentials of those in the back.

In this manner we passed through four German check posts; I was extremely relieved when we arrived at a house about five miles from Durazzo, where Halit Kola and I got out, leaving the others to drive on. At first light I set off with Halit to look at Durazzo. During the first hour we met and passed several German soldiers who took no notice of us; but suddenly, for no apparent reason, three German soldiers stopped us and asked for our identity cards. This was frankly embarrassing, firstly because I had none; secondly because my only weapon, a small automatic, was in my hip pocket, and I knew there was no round in the breech. Halit passed scrutiny, for he had the right documents, and moved on a few paces; I was glad to see him unsling his rifle as he did so. When it was my turn, all I could do was to repeat 'Un jam shqiptarë, skam dokument' ('I am an Albanian, I have no documents'). The German seemed undecided what to do, when Halit called to me 'Shkojm' ('Let us go'). I turned my back on the German and walked slowly away. To his horror, Halit saw the German quickly draw his pistol, lift it, and aim it at me. Then, shaking his head he lowered it, shrugged his shoulders, replaced it in his holster, and walked away. Halit told me this later and said he was so frozen with horror that he forgot the rifle in his hands — which may have been as well, for had he shot the German I doubt if I could have brought my automatic into action before the other Germans shot me.

After completing our reconnaissance we returned the same night to Shijak, to find Captain Tershana in a high state of alarm, saying that the Germans in Durazzo were arresting all Zogists and Ballists; he seemed keen for us to move, but Halit and I decided to stay in the house. Later that night, Major Drini arrived. 'You cannot leave tonight,' he gasped, jerking out the sentences as he strove to overcome his alarm. 'The Germans have cordoned the whole area, and they are searching all cars at their check points.' Rummaging in his suitcase, he pulled out a gendarme's uniform. 'Put that on,' he urged me. 'You will be safer in these clothes — as you are now, you don't look at all like an Albanian.'

I had very little sleep that night, not because of the Germans, but on account of my host, who was a *hoj*. Since this was the month of Ramadan, he spent the whole night either chanting prayers or beating a drum. Very early the next morning I got up and dressed in my new uniform, rather annoyed to note that I had been demoted to a corporal since the last time I had dressed as a gendarme. After the usual cup of hot milk, which served as breakfast, a truck arrived at the door, driven by a gendarme and with a gendarme sergeant beside him; and in the back was a German soldier. I climbed in front with the sergeant, Halit got in the back with the German, and we started off, stopping twice to pick up German soldiers who were hitchhiking. We were waved through four check points, presumably because we were in uniform and because of the Germans with us. At last we reached a village where Halit and I got out, watching the truck drive off with its German passengers.

After a seven-hour march we discovered that our HQ had moved to near the Ishm river; I bathed, changed back into British uniform, and gave McLean my news. My appreciation on the possibility of attacking Durazzo was disappointing, for it was my opinion that even if Kupi did capture it, he would be driven out with heavy losses within two days, by any German counterattack; he might well lose all his men, for Durazzo was on the sea, and they could have been completely cut off. We therefore decided to try and persuade Kupi to switch his attacks to dumps and roads.

The next day, Kupi arrived with good news. Some Turkestani troops had murdered their German officers and taken to the hills, and at least two thousand more were ripe for desertion; he added that thirty had already joined him. We therefore decided to move to a village as near to the Turkestani units as possible, taking our four Russians with us.

We found the Turkestani troops at this village, and from interrogation their past proved illuminating; they had murdered their Russian officers at Kharkov in 1942 and gone over to the Germans. Sent to the Balkans as garrison troops, they had grown discontent, for food was getting worse and they had received no pay for some time. They had made friends with a Zogist *boj*, for they too were Moslems, and he had encouraged them to desert; and so they had murdered their German officers and taken to the hills. Providing we could pay and feed them, they would be happy to serve us.

Disregarding the fate of their previous officers, we decided to employ them; for they had deserted with their arms, which were Russian, and could come in useful. They wore German uniform with the word 'Turkestan' on their shoulder titles, but this was not a very accurate description of them, for they were Tajiks, Kazaks, and Uzbeks. They had a very Asiatic appearance, especially the Kazaks who, with their round, cleanshaven faces and high cheekbones, looked completely Mongol.

Kupi had further good news. A German who worked in the Operations Room at Corps HQ in Tirana was willing to supply us with information in return for a safe conduct when the Germans quit Albania. Through a Zogist contact of Kupi's we accepted his offer. The first piece of information he produced was the complete German order of battle in Albania. This we were able to check with what we ourselves had discovered hitherto, and it seemed genuine. Later he produced the entire Order of Withdrawal of the Germans from the whole Balkan peninsula, some two weeks before the first moves took place, with photostatic copies of the orders and marked maps. We passed all this information to Bari, where we were told later that it was one of the best intelligence scoops of the war.

Next morning, I went off with the four Russians and two Tajiks to try to contact some more Turkestanis who we had heard were at a village in the area. We did not find them, but instead we discovered a German artillery unit, which we were told consisted of thirty Germans and thirty Italians, the latter being regarded as prisoners of the Germans; this seemed a good target, so I returned late that night to McLean, to report what I had seen.

Next morning, we had an interesting insight into the discipline of our new allies. A deputation turned up to say that they did not like their sergeant-major, who wanted to return to the Germans, and please could they have permission to shoot him? McLean smartly passed the buck back to them by saying that they must elect their own leaders, and that he would not interfere in these matters, whereupon they left us. Later in the day a shot rang out, followed by some wild singing and clapping. We went over to see what it was and found a circle of triumphant Turkestanis. In the centre of the circle lay their sergeant-major, shot in the back and twitching on the ground in his death throes. Describing this incident in his book, *Sons of the Eagle*, Amery concludes with a nice touch: 'and here I saw Sergeant Jones look meaningly at Sergeant Jenkins; for NCOs are also an international fraternity.'

We now had a *çeta* of more than a hundred Zogists attached to us, with Captain Ndue Pali in command, and Kupi's son Petrit with him. We also had about thirty Turkestanis, so we decided that an attack on the German camp would serve two purposes; it would prove whether or not the Turkestanis were willing to fight, and it would provide us with ample evidence to refute the LNÇ charges of Kupi's collaboration, which we suspected were accepted in Bari as true.

After we had made a daylight reconnaissance, we drew up a plan. The German camp consisted of a number of huts in the woods; it was well sheltered and camouflaged, out of the wind in a hollow, but was not well sited for defence, because it could be overlooked from the hills above and approached unseen from two directions. The plan, in brief, was for McLean with Petrit Kupi and a hundred Zogists to attack from one side, while Amery and the thirty Turkestanis attacked from the other; I would stay on the hill above with three machine guns to give covering fire, and a party of forty Zogists under Ndue Pali would be with me as a reserve, and to cover the withdrawal.

The execution of this operation left much to be desired and resulted in total confusion. McLean charged at the head of the Zogists, of whom Petrit Kupi and one other stayed with him, but the rest melted away. Amery led his Turkestanis in a rousing charge, in the course of which a bullet grazed his chin and knocked him down; my machine gunners fired into the barracks, and for a time Germans, Italians, Albanians, and Turkestanis joined in a mêlée, shooting in all directions and apparently without discriminating much between friend and foe. However, victory was ours, for the Germans fled, leaving ten dead on the ground. The camp was looted and burnt, and thirteen very frightened Italians were taken away with us to become prisoners of new masters.

We suffered casualties as well, for one Zogist and one Turkestani were killed, and one Zogist and one Turkestani wounded. We withdrew to our base and at once signalled to Bari that Zogist troops had attacked the Germans; but alas, it was too late, for two days later a signal from Bari arrived ordering McLean and myself to return to Italy soonest 'to report', leaving Amery to stay with Kupi. He was ordered not to encourage Kupi to fight, was informed that Kupi would receive no arms, and that Amery's attitude was to be that of a neutral observer.

The signal added that Hoxha had agreed that we should be 'escorted' to the coast for evacuation. We thought this sinister, and decided that if we left Albania it would *not* be through partisan hands; for even if we were not murdered, nothing would have given Hoxha greater pleasure than to parade us through his areas in the humiliating position of prisoners. This in fact happened to Simcox and Collins, who, after all their kit and equipment had been looted by the partisans, and their arms removed, were treated as prisoners, and marched south under conditions of the most calculated indignity. With Simcox was an Albanian, Lazar Fundo, who had been of great help to the mission; he had at one time been one of the first Soviet-trained propagators of Albanian Communism but had later defected. When Fundo was recognized, he was dragged before the commissar and beaten to death. This brutal murder was officially explained by Hoxha as 'execution for treason to the movement'.

There was only one thing to do about this signal: to procrastinate with Bari in carrying out its instructions, and ignore it in Albania; for our chances of fighting the Germans, who were beginning to pull out of the country, were at this moment higher than ever before. Not only were Kupi's men actually fighting the Germans, but Abas Ermenji, at the head of a thousand Ballists, had just appeared and offered us their services in the common cause, while the strength of our Turkestanis had risen to more than seventy, all of them well-armed.

Our own strength, apart from Concensus II (McLean, Amery and Smiley), included Merrett, Jones, Jenkins and Davis; the four Russians; and Franco and Mario with a party of Italians about a dozen strong. In addition, we had two American airmen with us. The first was Sergeant Corsentino, who had been with our mission for some months; he had bailed out of a Liberator that had crashed, but had soon decided that he preferred the life of a guerrilla to that of an airman. He had volunteered to stay with us in preference to evacuation, completing a trio with Jones and Jenkins, who both liked him, and became a useful member of our mission. The second was Staff Sergeant Shoemaker, who had bailed out of his crashing Liberator and had been brought to us by the Ballists, who had sheltered him for over a year.

We decided to split our forces, so that every party attacking the Germans should have a British adviser and, incidentally, someone to check the number of casualties inflicted on the enemy; for our experience with the partisans had proved their claims to be the wildest exaggerations, and signals from the

BLOs attached to them now suggested that they had not changed their methods. However, we found that the claims of the Zogists and Ballists were very accurate, and we always received captured German identity papers from them, which we never did from the partisans.

Our targets were to be Germans and their transport, with the object of destroying as many as possible and hindering their withdrawal in every way.

By now the increasing activity of RAF Beaufighters had forced the Germans to send all their transport columns by night, limiting their day traffic to single vehicles, so our ambushes were all to be after dark. For the two weeks starting on 9 September 1944, we gave little respite to the Germans travelling on the main Tirana-Scutari road.

To begin with a large Ballist *çeta*, commanded by Abas Ermenji, to whom Merrett, Jenkins and Corsentino were attached, attacked a German convoy on this main road, destroying fifteen vehicles, killing thirty-five Germans, and capturing much material.

On the next night Jenkins, accompanied by a Zogist *çeta*, mined the road and blew up three German vehicles. Then Jenkins and I, with a Zogist *çeta* and thirty Turkestanis, blew up a concrete bridge on the same road the following night. A German convoy was forced to halt, was fired on, and withdrew. Casualties were unknown.

On the night of 12-13 September, a combined force of Zogists and Ballists under Kupi and Ermenji, with McLean and Amery attached to them, attacked a German convoy of nine vehicles on this Tirana-Scutari road. All the vehicles were burnt and the Germans either fled or were killed, the dead including two officers. Much material was captured, including a bag of correspondence between the HQ of 181 Division and 21

Mountain Corps; this produced valuable intelligence later on. It was disappointing that the German convoy was so small, for there were 200 Zogists and 100 Ballists, and they had hoped for a bigger target.

The night after this I accompanied a *çeta* of twenty-five Zogists onto the Scutari road two miles outside Tirana and laid four Hawkins grenades at two different points. These devices could be used as a small mine; they would blow a wheel off but would not do much other damage. A German lorry went over one of the grenades, which stopped it, and we killed three Germans and destroyed the lorry by setting it on fire. An armoured car and a lorry full of troops came from Tirana to investigate the blaze and the shooting; another grenade exploded, and we had started to exchange fire with the armoured car and the troops who had scrambled out of the lorry, when suddenly a fusillade of shots came at us from behind. Thinking that we were being encircled, we gave the order to withdraw. We were followed up, however, and were thus able to identify the people who had been shooting at us from behind as partisans.

Our *çeta* now dispersed in some disorder. We lost touch with each other, and I found myself with only two men. When we got back to the village where I had left my mule, both the animal and the muleman had bolted, and the villagers were in a state of fear because the partisans were supposed to be near. I wanted to go north, but the two Albanians with me were so scared of partisans that they refused to come, and so I set off alone. I walked till nightfall avoiding villages, and then went in and asked for food and shelter; but on each occasion it was refused me because, although the occupants knew I was a British officer, they always answered the same: 'Kam frik partisana' ('I am afraid of the partisans'), and hurriedly shut the door in my face. The first night I slept for a couple of hours in the middle of a field of standing corn, for I was dead-beat; but it was bitterly cold, and I was only in shirt-sleeve order — my jacket and coat having been left on my mule.

The next day I found a boy, about twelve years old, who was very friendly and intelligent. He told me he knew where the partisans were, and by avoiding their posts we reached Luz. Thanking him with my last sovereign, I found two men in Luz who agreed to take me to Abas Kupi. I was very pleased that by now my Albanian was good enough to make myself understood, but after two hours' climb, I was furious when the two Albanians refused to take me any further without payment. Having no sovereigns left, I cursed them heartily in English and went on alone. The next village refused me food or shelter, but told me that partisan patrols had been in the area looking for the 'rebel English', whom they intended to shoot; so again I had to spend a night out, in some woods this time, but I was so cold I could not sleep.

I had now gone for two days without food; I was in shirtsleeves, had had very little sleep, and altogether was pretty cold and miserable, but my determination to avoid the partisans kept me going. Next day I set off north again, following a mule track on the side of the mountain, and finally came to a village where, by extraordinary good luck, I found a Zogist *çeta*, and with them, to my delight, were McLean and Amery. When I had swallowed some food, and washed and shaved, I told McLean my adventures; then I quickly fell asleep, only to be woken far too soon, to be told that we were on the move again because partisan patrols were reported to be half-an-hour away.

The details of my last action were signalled to Bari in due course. For partisans to attack a Zogist *çeta* engaged in action against the Germans was proof enough of their intentions, but the staff in our Bari office were not impressed; to their warped minds Kupi was the collaborator, and the LNÇ our true allies.

While I had been on the run, McLean, Amery and Jenkins, with a mixed force of Zogists and Turkestanis, had attacked a German armoured car patrol, and forced it to retreat.

We gave the Germans a rest for two nights before Jenkins and Shoemaker with a mixed Zogist and Ballist *çeta* blew up a bridge on the Tirana-Scutari road, and destroyed one German truck. The following night they attacked a German convoy on the same road, forcing it to withdraw, with an unknown number of casualties.

My final action was with a Zogist *çeta* and some Turkestanis. We blew up the bridge at Han i Teqes, and attacked a German convoy, forcing it back.

In these two weeks it can be seen that we were very active with both Zogists and Ballists killing Germans. But it was clear by now that any further large-scale actions against the Germans by ourselves or Abas Kupi were finished, and we turned our thoughts to evacuation. As the Bari office was still — incredibly — insisting that we handed ourselves over to the partisans, we decided to get hold of a boat of our own. So Toptani went to Scutari to enquire about them, while I went on a reconnaissance of the coast between the mouths of the Drin and Mati rivers. I left by night, taking Halit with me, and we filled our pockets with tyre-bursters, which we laid on the main road as we crossed it. We heard a bang sometime later, but pushed on to the coast, where after some hours' walk we reached the house of a fisherman, whom Halit knew. He gave us a wonderful lunch, for a sucking-pig was brought in and killed, cleaned, cooked, and finally eaten all in the same room.

Our host was a Catholic, but Halit, being a Moslem, would not eat the pig.

After lunch we went to the sea. There was no sign of Germans, and the steeply sloping sandy beach looked as though the Navy would approve it for our evacuation. We left the next night and, crossing the main road just before first light, we laid the rest of our tyre-bursters on its surface. After climbing up a track for some minutes, we reached a house and sat down outside while our host brought us coffee. As dawn was breaking a convoy of about twenty vehicles approached, and the first one ran over a tyre-burster. The convoy halted, and Germans piled out and immediately opened a furious fire on a wood situated on the side of the mountain about four hundred yards from us, bringing both machine guns and mortars into action. Halit and I sat drinking our coffee and enjoying the firework display; but eventually the Germans moved on and we did likewise, joining up with McLean, Amery, Kupi and a large following at the village of Mai i Bardhë.

We stayed there several days and had a succession of important visitors. The first was Fiqri Dine, who had been the German-sponsored Prime Minister, but had now taken to the mountains. He gave McLean and Amery a frank account of his past activities and his motives, and he was now optimistically hoping that he could join the Nationalists and the Gheg chieftains to form an alliance against the partisans. He left the next day.

With Fiqri Dine came General Prenk Prevesi, accompanied by his staff and sixty Albanian soldiers, all in uniform and armed. Prevesi had been, and I suppose still was, Commander-in-Chief of the Albanian Army. He was very well turned out, and his highly polished black field boots looked somewhat out of place in the mountains, but at least he had removed his spurs. The extreme deference of his staff, and his military airs and postures, brought a touch of comedy to the atmosphere. I warmed towards him during the weeks he and his soldiers were with us, and his men proved valuable escorts and guards.

The Ballist leaders Mid'hat Frashëri and Ali Këlcyra also came to see us, and had a number of long discussions with McLean and Amery; I made myself scarce on these occasions for my interest in Albanian politics, never strong, had waned since it now seemed to me that, whatever plans they might make, the result was a foregone conclusion. They left with Fiqri Dine, but they came to see us again before we left Albania.

Another newcomer was a staunch Zogist, Gaqo Gogo, a former Minister of Sport in King Zog's day and himself an Olympic athlete. He remained with us for the rest of our stay in Albania, acting as secretary and interpreter to Kupi. He was a most entertaining companion, and his high spirits and sense of fun helped to maintain my morale when it flagged sometimes; so did the nightly dancing and singing by the Turkestanis round the campfires.

During the following three weeks we marched and countermarched, always keeping one jump ahead of the partisans, who were very persistent in their attempts to track us down. We were a numerous party, for, besides our own personal retainers and camp followers, there was a large *çeta* of Kupi's, more than eighty Turkestanis, the four Russians, a party of Italians, and General Prenk Prevesi with some sixty of his soldiers. A body of this size was of doubtful advantage as far as security was concerned, for it could not easily be concealed, and our presence was always known to the partisans before long; on the other hand, our strength was such that we could easily beat off any patrol that might try to attack us. However, the chief reason for our continual moves was to sidestep involvement in any major action; moreover, we had received orders from Bari at all costs to avoid opening fire on partisan patrols.

While we were at Mai i Bardhë, Jenkins and I twice went down to the main road and blew up a bridge; I suspect McLean let us go to stop us from becoming bored. We took great interest in the Zog bridge, which carried the main Scutari-Tirana road over the Mati River, for it was the biggest bridge in Albania. Unfortunately it was very heavily guarded, a battalion of Germans being in the area, and so our desire to blow it up was little more than wishful thinking; but it was very tantalizing, especially as I could even see the demolition chambers through my binoculars.

One of Ihsan Toptani's mulemen had just returned to him after being captured by the partisans near Tirana. He had been mercilessly tortured and beaten to make him reveal the whereabouts of our mission, and reveal it the poor man did, which accounted for the partisan attack on our camp in the olive grove. His main item of information was of considerable personal interest, for the partisans had told him they had orders to shoot McLean and Smiley on the spot.

This was at a time when we were still receiving signals from Bari ordering us to cross to the partisan lines and give ourselves up for evacuation. When we finally reached Bari, we demanded from the head of our section an explanation of the purpose behind this order; we received the astounding reply that it was 'to test Enver Hoxha's good faith'.

On 27 September we heard cheering news on the BBC, to the effect that British troops had landed in Albania. We were all thrilled, thinking that this was the start of our reoccupation of the Balkans, and we had great difficulty in dissuading the Albanians from firing off a *feu de joie*; Kupi, also, talked of marching off with his men to fight alongside the British troops. We had no news of this landing from Bari for two days. Our hopes were dashed when we heard it was only a commando raid.

Two days later, we were warned of approaching partisans and moved north again, crossing the Mati and Fani rivers by night. They were both flowing very fast and the water came up to our waists. We linked arms and struggled across the fierce current in parties of twenty. We had great trouble with the mules, but in the end ferried them all across safely, though they finished up several hundred yards downstream. With more rain the river would rise considerably, and this would put a forbidding obstacle between the partisans and ourselves.

Our new base was in the village of Veljë, lying high up on the slopes of a mountain of the same name, where we made our quarters in the house of the local Catholic priest. The only disadvantage was two big church bells in the garden, which were rung at all hours of the day and night. The town of Lesh (Alessio) was two hours' walk away and though it had a German garrison, it was reputed to be a good shopping town, and so we were able to keep ourselves well supplied by sending couriers.

McLean felt rather ill during the next few days with what he thought was neuralgia; I suspected that he needed a tooth pulling out, but there was nothing to be done about it. In general, we were all very lucky in our health, for we seldom needed a doctor. Both McLean and Amery were constitutionally tough, and never suffered from anything worse than the odd tummy trouble or a touch of fever. I was tough enough too, though I seemed to have more than my fair share of malaria; this was probably due to the irregularity with which we took our atabrine pills, for they would often run out or we would lose them all, as we did when the partisans overran our HQ in the olive grove.

Local doctors were almost impossible to find, but two cures tried out on me were very effective. Once I had a very bad headache, and Asslan said he would cure me, for being a *hoj* he claimed special powers. First of all, he wrote out a prayer in Arabic and put the piece of paper in one of my hands. He then held my hand between his while he muttered prayers in Arabic for about five minutes. After this he blew hard twice into my right ear. The headache went immediately. This is true and the cure most effective, though I have no explanation to offer.

Another treatment was being 'cupped'. I was stripped to the waist and laid on my front, while a number of what looked like egg cups were placed at intervals on my back. These had previously had cotton wool burned in them, and their heat created a vacuum. As a result, my back was drawn up into the cups in large red hemispherical lumps. After these had been massaged I felt much better. The treatment was normally applied to the aches and pains that accompanied malaria.

While at Veljë I carried out a reconnaissance of Lesh. Wearing civilian clothes, I went into the town with Halit, and later signalled Bari some possible targets for RAF attack. We also set up a road-watching post overlooking the main road near Lesh, which our NCOs took turns to man. We signalled Bari all the big German convoy movements in the hopes that an RAF strike could be mounted. Mario and Franco took turns at this vigil as well as going into Lesh to contact Italians there.

I made a much longer reconnaissance when I went with Shaqir to Shëngjin, a small port and the most northerly in Albania, only twelve miles or so from the frontier with

Montenegro. Having crossed the River Drin in a canoe made from a hollowed tree trunk, climbed two mountain ranges, waded through a marsh and then rowed across a lake, we ended up spending the night in a shepherd's hut.

In the morning we had a fine view of Shëngjin and the port, but I was unable to enter the town because it was a protected area with check points, and I had no identity card. I marked the German positions on my map but doubted if the information would be of much use, because the Germans would probably have gone by the time I had reached Bari. We returned the way we had come and bought some fish and eels from the boatman who ferried us over the lake.

The next day we lunched with Bishop Bumçi, who had been Bishop of Mirditë for thirty-five years, and at one time Regent of Albania. In spite of his age and ill health he had a remarkably active and penetrating mind, asking me many pointed and at times awkward questions. He was quite annoyed with me when he heard that I was the one responsible for the destruction of Gjole bridge, for it had interfered with his food supplies. He gave me an excellent lunch, made even more enjoyable by the two lovely girls who waited on us. Before I left, the bishop said he was quite sure the Allies had already decided the future of Albania, and that it was going to be a Russian sphere of influence; I had a feeling he might be right.

On my return to Veljë I found the camp in some state of excitement, for a German patrol had approached our base, exchanged shots with the Zogist guards, and, as others had joined in, beaten a hasty retreat. It was believed that they had bumped into us by accident, while searching for a band of gendarmes who had deserted the night before.

One day towards the end of our stay in Veljë we climbed the mountain, over 3500 feet high, and from the top had magnificent views. Kupi and some of his bodyguard came too; it was to be the last time that any of us would be able to gaze over the rugged and forbidding mountains that we now knew so well and had grown so fond of.

While we were at Veljë, Ihsan Toptani arrived with the news of a boat he was negotiating for in Scutari. It was available, if more money was forthcoming. On 13 October, however, two weeks after we had arrived at Veljë, we received the awaited signal from Bari. They had at last agreed to evacuate us by sea, and so we made plans to move to the coast as soon as possible. We said our farewells and expressed our thanks to General Prevesi and his officers. He knew he would not be able to come with us, but as he was in his own tribal area, at least he had some hope of safety.

We descended to the plain and crossed the main road in the dark at the exact moment when a German armoured car chose to appear. The shambles was terrific, for over a hundred of us were on the road at the time and we scattered in all directions — I happened to be riding a mule, and it charged through a brick wall, damaging my knee. However, the Germans were probably equally surprised and decided to beat a prudent retreat; slamming down their turret they drove past us at a high speed, and not a shot was fired by either side.

A gruelling march with no halts and lasting for fourteen hours brought us to a wood in the plains, where we rested; then we moved on to a large house standing alone in the middle of a wide plain, broken by a few scattered trees. This was to be our last base before leaving Albania. The house was owned by two wealthy brothers, who were old friends of Kupi's. It was about two hours' march from the sea, but it was not a place where we could afford to linger, for our party was still over 200 strong. Once the partisans knew where we were, we should have little chance of escape. It was ironic that our main thoughts were now of an attack by the partisans, our former colleagues, rather than the usual threat from the Germans.

On our first day there we heard that Neel and his party had been evacuated from a point on the coast quite near to where we had made our reconnaissance. This was encouraging, but it was accompanied by tragic news; his excellent operator, Corporal Button, who had been in the country for over a year, had been drowned when the dinghy taking him out to the MTB had overturned. We were asked to go and search for his body, because he was carrying his code books on him, and in German hands they could compromise others. Jenkins and I set off for the coast, not only to look for Button's body, but to seek out a place for our own evacuation. We found a suitable beach, and signalled the details to Bari, but there was no sign of Button's body. Mid'hat Frashëri and Ali Këlcyra came to see us shortly after, and Frashëri told us that it had been found by the Germans.

A signal from Bari had informed us that Hibberdine was in Scutari with paratyphoid, in the care of an Italian doctor; in due course he joined us, looking far from well but still under the care of the doctor, who came with him.

While we were waiting for the boat, McLean was carrying out an acrimonious exchange of signals with Bari. Bari had sent a signal insisting that only the British were to be evacuated. Our reactions to this order were of consternation and dismay. Our friend and ally Abas Kupi; our loyal interpreters Shaqir, Halit and Veli and the two Italians, Franco and Mario, who had been with us so long — none of these, for whom McLean had especially asked for evacuation, would be allowed to accompany us. The humiliation at such treachery in leaving these people, to some of whom we owed our lives, to the mercies of the partisans was intolerable; but all pleas and reasoned arguments by McLean were rejected. As a final resort, on 25 October McLean availed himself of the offer to send a personal signal to the Foreign Secretary. Mr Eden never received this signal; on my return to Bari, I discovered that it had been deliberately suppressed in the SOE office.

While some of the officers in the Albanian section of the SOE office were well-intentioned, if led astray by insidious Communist propaganda, others were Communist agents. One was an officer in the Albanian Section, and I was told he stood as an unsuccessful Communist candidate in the 1945 election. It was not surprising that on our return I overheard him refer to our mission as 'Fascists'. I was told by one of the secretaries that it was he who had prevented further transmission of McLean's signal to Mr Eden, and that he had deliberately disposed of the message.

To this day I am ashamed of this abandonment of our friends. On our return we learnt that our orders to do so were simply to appease Enver Hoxha and his fellow murderers; this made our feelings more bitter.

Our departure is a bad memory of the sad farewells to those of our friends who knew the secret that we were going. On security grounds we had to conceal it from the others, slipping off at night without a word.

Our evacuation was to be carried out by two boats on consecutive nights, and so we were divided into two parties. On the first night both boats arrived, which could easily have evacuated everyone at once, but this was not what Bari had ordered. The first party to leave, with myself in charge, consisted of Merrett, Jones, Jenkins, Corsentino, Shoemaker, and a very lucky pilot of a Spitfire of the South African Air

Force. He had crashed only two days before and had been found by two of Kupi's men.

The two boats were of the Italian MAS type (a sort of ML) with Italian crews under Commander Tony de Cosson RN. One boat took all our party aboard, while the other disembarked a patrol from the Long Range Desert Group which had come to carry out operations against the withdrawing Germans. We reached Brindisi after an uneventful trip of eight hours, and I drove to Bari as soon as I could.

The following night McLean, Amery, Hibberdine, and Davis were successfully picked up, and as a last-minute concession the four Russians and two Turkestanis were allowed to go too — presumably because this would not offend Enver Hoxha. Such was the distrust of us held in the Bari office that a special security officer was sent with the boats to ensure that we made no last-minute attempt to bring our friends with us.

On arrival at Bari we were politely treated in the SOE office, though we felt an undercurrent of hostility. To secure the evacuation of Kupi was now the only purpose in our minds, and as the policy of the SOE office appeared to be dictated entirely by partisan interests, there was little sympathy or likely help for Kupi; we had to look elsewhere for support. Having found out the fate of McLean's signal to the Foreign Secretary we therefore sent him another urgent one, to which Mr Eden replied at once, recommending that Kupi be evacuated. The SOE office stalled, pleading that they had to receive firm orders, so McLean and Amery flew to Caserta, the HQ of General Wilson, our Supreme Commander in Italy, where they saw both the General and Mr Harold Macmillan, the Resident Minister of State. They both agreed at once that Kupi must be rescued, and General Wilson promptly gave the orders to his staff. McLean and Amery returned to Bari, happy with the result, but anxious whether rescue could come in time.

They need not have worried. While Kupi's fate was being decided in London and Caserta, events on the other side of the Adriatic were taking a turn for the better. Ihsan Toptani's negotiations for a boat had at last borne fruit, and a Montenegrin had picked up Kupi and his two sons, and Gaqo Gogo, Toptani, and my friend Ramiz. The engine had failed in the middle of the Adriatic and for six days they had drifted helplessly, out of food and water, and had almost given up hope when they were sighted by a British minesweeper and towed into Brindisi.

We went down to greet them; they were now housed in a sparsely furnished villa under a guard, but we knew that they were safe. They were joined there a few days later by Said Kryeziu, who had been brought out from the south; Alan Hare had been evacuated from the partisan area, so our party was safely reunited. But the fate of those left behind was still unknown.

The attitude of the authorities in Bari shook us badly; of course, the Russians were our allies at this stage of the war, but it seemed incomprehensible that senior British officers could not understand the simplest principles of Communism. On one of our first nights there, Amery was talking about Tito to the senior officer responsible for mounting all operations in the Balkans. Amery described him as a loyal agent of the Comintern, to which this worthy officer replied that Stalin had dissolved the Comintern two years ago; Amery ventured to disagree, and received the reply, 'Anyone would think that you had been listening to Goebbels.'

We remained a week at Bari, writing reports, being interviewed, and visiting Kupi and his companions at the villa in Rutigliano. At the end of the week we said goodbye to our friends, delighted to learn that an attempt by Hoxha to have them returned to Albania for trial had been rejected. McLean and Amery flew direct to London, while I returned to Cairo for three weeks.

Back in Cairo, the old familiar round of parties and other social activities was unchanged. I stayed at Tara, where I found Sophie had become engaged to Billy Moss; Xan Fielding and Paddy Leigh Fermor were not there, and the atmosphere of Tara had lost its sense of fun. I busied myself in winding up all my Middle East and Balkan affairs, before returning to England.

After the war, both McLean and Amery fulfilled their ambitions of standing for Parliament. McLean, who was awarded a DSO for his activities in Albania, served as Conservative Member for Inverness from 1954 to 1966. Even then he seemed drawn back to his former guerrilla life. He was the first British MP to visit the Algerians when they were fighting the French; he also paid a number of visits to the Yemen and the mountain strongholds where the Imam was conducting a guerrilla war against Nasser's Egyptian troops.

Amery became Conservative Member of Parliament for Preston in 1962 and held a number of ministerial appointments. He was Minister of Aviation in 1962. He lost his seat in the 1966 election, but got elected again, this time for Brighton, in a by-election in 1969, and was a member until 1992.

Kemp, who also ended the war with a DSO, later worked as an insurance consultant; he has written several successful books, essays and newspaper articles. Duffy returned to the

Royal Engineers and Seymour continued as a regular officer until he died on duty in the Far East.

Of the wireless officers, Collins has recently retired from employment in the Civil Service, and Davis (Çuni) emigrated to New Zealand. I have lost touch with Jenkins, last seen when he came to my wedding.

Of Trotsky's Mission, Trotsky himself, after many adventures as a prisoner of war, ended up at the fortress prison of Colditz, where he made himself an unmitigated nuisance to the Germans. I last saw him when he came to lecture at the Senior Officers' School, where I was a student. He had recovered from his wounds and was engaged in writing a book of his experiences; he never lived to see it published, for he died of a heart attack in camp in Wales while commanding a Territorial Brigade. The book, *Illyrian Adventure*, was published after his death. Alan Hare, his Staff Captain, became Chairman of the *Financial Times*.

It is difficult to get news out of Albania, although it does filter through occasionally, by way of refugees who have escaped or through BBC monitoring reports. Most of the details that follow have been gleaned from my Albanian friends in exile, or from various newsletters that I continue to receive from free Albanian political movements.

Of those in the partisan movement, Enver Hoxha and Mehmet Shehu became the leaders of Communist Albania. They have fallen out with Russia and China and appear to have no friends outside the country.

When we left Albania in 1944 Enver Hoxha was the military commander of the LNÇ, and had already assumed the rank of Lieutenant-General; in 1946 he became Prime Minister and Minister for Foreign Affairs, and, in 1945 President of Albania, which he remained until his death in 1985. In 1944 Mehmet

Shehu was promoted to Major-General; in 1945, after attending the Voroshilov Military Academy in Moscow, he became Chief of Staff to the Albanian Army; in 1948 he fell from power because of his anti-Tito views.

However, at the time of the Tito-Cominform break he escaped being purged, and returned to favour as Minister of the Interior; in 1954 he succeeded Enver Hoxha as Prime Minister, and still held that position until he was reported as having committed suicide in 1981. Later he was denounced by Enver Hoxha as a double agent for both the Americans and Yugoslavs. He was most likely executed.

Bedri Spahiu was promoted Major-General in 1944, and the following year was Public Prosecutor at the Special Court set up to try Albanians alleged to be 'war criminals and enemies of the people'.

This was a period when thousands of Albanians were executed or sent to concentration camps on such charges, with or without trial. The majority of these unfortunate people were merely political opponents in the Communist regime. In 1948 Bedri Spahiu became State Public Prosecutor and, in 1955, Minister of Education; but he was purged in the same year.

Dr Ymer Dishnica became Minister of Health in 1944 but was later purged. Kahreman Ylli was purged in 1952, after he had been Envoy to France in 1946 and Minister of Education in 1948.

Baba Faja is dead, killed by the Supreme Head of the Bektashi Sect, Dede Baba Abazi. It appears that a religious discussion between these two and another priest turned into a heated argument; Baba Abazi drew his pistol and shot both Baba Faja and the other priest, and then turned the pistol on himself and committed suicide.

The likeable old rogue Mestan Ujaniku soon fell out with the Communists and was hanged. Gjin Marku was promoted Major-General in 1949 and was executed in a 1950 purge. Nexhip Vinçani was said to be purged in 1952, but may have regained favour, because he was reported as Commandant of the Durazzo garrison from 1954-7. Petrit Dume, already a General, was appointed Commander in Chief of the Albanian Army in 1962 but purged later, then executed. Fred Nosi was President of the Military Tribunal, which in 1949, tried Koçi Xoxe, the former Minister of the Interior. He sentenced him to death.

Kochi Tashko, alias Shander Dine was purged in 1960, as was Rita Marko — my so-called bodyguard when at Shtyllë and Leshnjë. Mustapha Ginishi was shot on orders of Enver Hoxha. Dali Ndreu was shot in the late 1940s on suspicion of having contact with the Yugoslavs.

It can be seen that few of our contemporaries with the partisans have retired quietly; some are now serving in high positions, others have been purged or imprisoned, and many have been executed. Such is the way of life in a Communist country.

A number of our Albanian friends have escaped into exile and are scattered all over the world. Abas Kupi settled in New York where he died in 1977; his son Petrit settled in Australia, then moved to New York where he still lives. His bodyguard Ramiz Dani, my companion of many adventures, accompanied Kupi to New York, but Bardhok, who shared them with us, was killed by the partisans. Abas Kupi was passing through London in 1961, on his way back from King Zog's funeral. I met him in White's Club; he had not changed much, and we embraced each other warmly. I could not help being amused to notice that there was still the familiar bulge in his hip pocket.

Gaqo Goga, who escaped in the boat with Kupi, is now working with a news agency in New York, and has changed his name to George Gogh.

Abas Ermenji escaped to Greece and lives in Paris now, where he is the leader of the Balli Kombëtar in exile and actively involved in politics, since he is President of the National Democratic Committee for a Free Albania and a member of the International Executive Council of the European Movement. General Prenk Prevesi and Muharrem Bajraktari both managed to elude the partisans and escape to Greece.

Ihsan Toptani was granted British citizenship and worked for the monitoring service of the BBC, and now lives in London. He came to stay with me in Scotland, when he gave me valuable help with the spelling of Albanian names and words used in this book.

Of the Kryeziu brothers, Said is a banker in New York and married there. Hasan was executed by Tito, and Gani was sentenced to five years hard labour. He was released after serving his sentence, but his family have had no further news from him and fear the worst.

Of our interpreters Shaqir Trimi, Veli Hassan, and Halit Kola there is no recent news. It is not known whether Shaqir was released after serving his fifteen years hard labour, and the last news of Halit Kola was that he was killed in the mountains while leading a *çeta* against the Communists.

Chapter XI: Postscript on Albania

I had returned to England at the end of 1945 and, after a skiing holiday in Switzerland, went to the Staff College. On qualifying, I was appointed Assistant Military Attaché to our Embassy in Warsaw. After some months I was declared *persona non grata* for alleged spying and returned to London. There I was recruited by an old friend, Brigadier Bernard Fergusson, to join him in Palestine to train the Palestine Police in paramilitary methods. I was by now engaged to be married, and on learning that wives were not allowed to accompany husbands on this assignment I asked to cry off. Instead I was seconded to MI6 for a year, at the end of which I returned to my regiment, the Blues, in Germany as second-in-command.

While I was in Germany, I was contacted by two friends in MI6 who asked me if I would be willing to return for a special assignment, to which I agreed.

In July 1949, I went to London to start my secondment to MI6. I was briefed by an old friend, Colonel Harold Perkins — known to his friends as Perks. He had been a senior officer in the Polish section of SOE during the war. After the war ended and SOE was finally wound up, only very few SOE people were taken on by MI6, and many old SOE hands got the impression that they regarded us as a lot of bungling amateurs.

During my previous secondment to MI6, I had not only been under the orders of Perks for certain operations, but he insisted on joining me for the more hazardous and exciting missions. Perks was a big man, full of fun and not only a brave and congenial companion on operations, but also a leader for whom it was a pleasure to work.

Perks told me that the situation in Albania was very fluid: the Communists under Enver Hoxha and Mehmet Shehu had gained control of most of the country, thanks entirely to the arms sent to them by SOE and not, as their history books now show, due to Russia, though they received moral support from Tito in Yugoslavia. However, there were still pockets of resistance where members of the Balli Kombëtar and the followers of Abas Kupi's Legality Movement had taken to the mountains and were fighting the Communists. If these groups could be contacted and helped with arms and money, they might have a chance of thwarting the Communist takeover.

At this time a Russian-inspired civil war was being fought in Greece, and Russia had a good chance of securing her long wished-for base in the Mediterranean. The Greek Communists were receiving their supplies through both Yugoslavia and Albania. It would clearly be in the interests of the West if the Albanian conduit could be blocked. On these points the British and Americans were in agreement, and a joint operation in Albania was planned whereby the two countries would cooperate in sponsoring any of those Albanians who were actively opposed to the Communists and would work together towards the overthrow of a regime which was supported by only a minority of the Albanian population.

Whereas at the end of the war SOE was completely disbanded, and MI6 carried on in its customary role of the British Secret Service, the Americans were different. Before the war they had no secret service as we know it, and during the war General 'Wild Bill' Donovan initiated the OSS (Office of Strategic Services) which functioned through the latter years of the war in a similar role to SOE. After the war ended, the OSS was gradually transformed into the Central Intelligence Agency. As far as the Albanian operations were concerned, the joint committee that had been set up decided that the Americans would be responsible for operations in the north of Albania, infiltrating most of their agents by parachute, while the British would operate in the south, sending agents in by sea.

I was to set up a training school for Albanians in Malta, and once satisfied that they were well-trained organize their landing on the coast of Albania. It was hoped that they would make their way inland to contact their friends and relatives who, together with those already fighting, would form the nucleus of active opposition to the Communists. They were to be trained in radio operating so that they could report back to us the situation in the country.

I flew out to Malta in the spring, to set up a training depot for the Albanians who would arrive later. As this was a top-secret operation, only a very few senior officers in Malta were in the know and my own cover was the first problem. And once this was established, how was I to train a number of Albanians in such a small island as Malta? The first problem was solved by the General commanding the island agreeing to my becoming the Deputy Chief of Staff in the Malta garrison. The Chief of Staff had to be let into the secret, but these were the only two military men in the know. As the Royal Navy would be involved later, the senior admiral, and his senior intelligence officer were kept informed. Although Malta was then a colony and had a governor who was commander-in-chief, as far as I was aware the only other person informed of my activities was the MI5 man in Malta, Major Bill Major (Major by rank and Major by name). He was not only of the greatest help in keeping the cover of the Albanians who eventually arrived, but also in dealing with the customs over the equipment that was sent out, such as sub-machine guns, pistols and wireless sets. For this he had on his staff a splendid Maltese 'Man Friday' called George, who wore the uniform of a sergeant in the Malta Police.

First, accommodation for the Albanians had to be found, and then their cover had to be invented. Fort Benjimma, built during the Napoleonic wars, fitted the bill. Standing in wild country on the far side of Medina and away from the more populous area of Valetta, it could be approached only by a rough track. There was ample sleeping space for the Albanians and my staff, plenty of storerooms, and the moat round the fort made an ideal firing range. As the Albanians would obviously object to being incarcerated in the fort and would like to visit at times the fleshpots of Valetta and other parts of Malta, they needed a cover in case they were picked up by the police. So they were put into British battledress with Pioneer Corps flashes on their shoulders. (After the war a great many displaced persons in Germany — many of them Poles, Czechs, Yugoslavs and others who had no wish to return home — were employed by the occupying forces, so it would not, therefore, be too suspicious if our Albanians were discovered.) Luckily they were never in trouble. They were not mere conscripts, but brave patriots who had volunteered to risk their lives in their hopes of liberating their country from a hated tyranny. As far as I knew there was only one breach of discipline, when some of them were picked up in Valetta by the Military Police for wearing gym shoes with their battledress, but this was quietly sorted out by Bill Major. They always wore gym shoes on training, and when finally put ashore in Albania some still insisted on wearing them with their civilian clothes.

The Albanians who came to Malta were either recruited by General Abas Kupi, the leader of the Legality Movement and a staunch supporter of the exiled King Zog, or by Professor Abas Ermenji, leader of the Balli Kombëtar, the Nationalist party which, though not in favour of King Zog, sank its differences with the Zogists in their mutual hatred of Communism. I also had three excellent Albanian interpreters and a British staff made up of a weapon training officer, two wireless operators, a quartermaster, and a don from Oxford, Professor Zaehner. 'Doc' Zaehner, as we called him, was a brilliant scholar in classical Persian, and although he was sent as an interpreter, his own speciality and Albanian had little in common, but he was a most useful and entertaining member of the staff. The two wireless operators not only trained the Albanians in the use of wireless sets and codes; they also operated the set that kept me in touch with my HQ in London. Among the operators, I was very lucky to have Sergeant 'Gunner' Collins as one of them; he had not only served in Albania with SOE but had been my personal operator in Siam in 1945. He got on well with the Albanians and was a real friend of mine.

As all my signals to and from London had to be in code I needed a cipher clerk, so my wife Moy, who had been an experienced wartime FANY cipher officer, did a refresher course in London. In Malta she was responsible for all the cipher work at the fort.

The course consisted of weapon training with pistols and sub-machine guns, wireless and PT. The wireless sets were the type used by SOE during the war, but instead of a heavy battery and charging engine — clearly too heavy for anyone to carry on this operation — a type of collapsible bicycle without wheels was used to power the sets, one man pedalling away busily while they were sending out signals. The PT was essential, as most of the Albanians had come from camps in

Italy and needed toughening up to tackle the arduous mountain tracks of their home. Apart from walks over the local hills, they also had plenty of chances to bathe in a local and almost deserted bay.

Security meant that Moy and I had a far from easy life. As deputy chief of staff — I had been promoted to lieutenant-colonel again for the job — I clocked in regularly at the garrison HQ in the Castille, a delightful old building in use since the days of the Knights of Malta. After collecting and reading my mail, I would spend about an hour in the Castille trying to be seen by as many people as possible, then get in my car and drive off to the fort where I spent the rest of the morning. As summer hours were in force, there was no reason to return to the Castille in the afternoon, so I could spend the rest of the day either at the fort or at leisure.

As Malta is a small island, and there was a lot of social life, we had to play our part if we were not to arouse suspicion by being continually absent. So I took up polo again with delight — I had last gone in for it at Windsor before the war — and played regularly at the Marsa Club four days a week, among the players being Earl Mountbatten and Prince Philip, who was a beginner at the game in those days. Princess Elizabeth was living in Malta at the time, and I was told she was keen to play polo too, but her uncle discouraged this since he was apprehensive of the heir to the throne risking injury.

By midsummer, the Albanians were well enough trained and the weather right for operations to start. They had been formed into small groups agreed among themselves, depending on their politics, relations, tribes and the areas from which they came. Each group, of four to six men, had a wireless set. The plan was to put them ashore at the point in Albania from which McLean and I had been evacuated in 1943 — a rocky area of steep cliffs with the odd inlet where a boat could beach, from where goat tracks led inland. They would then move inland to the tribal areas where they had friends and relatives and would signal back the state of the country and the chances of further operations to help those already fighting the Communists.

The groups left Malta at intervals in a motor fishing vessel (MFV) manned by men of the Royal Navy. In the Adriatic they were switched to a Greek caique run by two British officers who put them ashore at night. This part of the operation went smoothly. At no time were the ships discovered.

Once all the groups had been put ashore, the station at Malta closed down and I moved to Greece. This time my cover was GI (Ops & I) with the British military mission. Moy and I lived on the sea at Glyfada, about ten miles from Athens. We had a safe house nearby for any Albanians who might return. Our wireless base was set up on Corfu.

Days went by without any news. Then one or two groups made contact to say that they had run into trouble early on and hinted that they might have been expected. This was confirmed later by members of the groups who had managed to work their way overland into Greece, where they were promptly jailed by the Greeks who very reluctantly released them in due course. They seemed absolutely convinced that their enemies had been waiting for them, for some groups had found themselves ambushed and had sustained casualties almost immediately after leaving the beach. We therefore faced the very unpleasant fact that there had either been a breach of security, or a traitor.

Once all the groups had been accounted for, my job was over and I returned to my regiment in Germany, very downcast and completely mystified as to what had gone wrong.

I did not find out until I read Kim Philby's *My Silent War* in 1968. When Philby defected in 1963, the truth became obvious at once to people in MI6; but I was no longer connected with them and did not relate Philby to the Albanian operation, as I did not know what he had been doing in Washington.

According to Philby's own account, he had to deal with two divisions of the CIA on behalf of MI6. One was the Office of Strategic Operations (OSO) and the other the Office of Policy Co-ordination (OPC). It was mainly with the OPC that Philby liaised over Albania. He was based in Washington, but he made several flying visits to Greece and Italy, and though he does not admit it in his book, he was quite certainly telling the Russians all the details of the operations I was running from Malta, and no doubt the Russians were passing everything on to Enver Hoxha. This traitor therefore caused the failure of our Albanian operations, and the deaths of many brave and patriotic Albanians.

Today Albania has no friends, having fallen out with both the Russians and the Chinese. With hostile Greeks and Yugoslavs on their borders they are completely isolated, and life there must indeed be grim. One can only hope that the day will come when Albania will be free. But one may be certain that so ancient, stubborn, courageous and freedom-loving a nation will not endure Communist domination forever.

Acknowledgements

This book would not have been written had I not been encouraged to write it by a very good friend — Brigadier Bernard Fergusson (the late Lord Ballantrae) who had seen some of my diaries. Peter Kemp checked the first draft, and subsequent criticisms and corrections were made by Paddy Leigh Fermor, my wife Moy and my son Xan to whom I owe a great debt of thanks for their help and patience. I would also like to thank Ihsan Toptani who gave me advice on Albanian names of people and places.

Finally Mrs Irma Harwood, who did all the typing, and her husband Stuart; they took infinite trouble to produce an accurate and faultlessly typed script.

If you have enjoyed this book enough to leave a review on Amazon and Goodreads, then we would be truly grateful.

The Estate of David Smiley

Sapere Books is an exciting new publisher of brilliant fiction and popular history.

To find out more about our latest releases and our monthly bargain books visit our website:
saperebooks.com

Printed in Great Britain
by Amazon